First World War
and Army of Occupation
War Diary
France, Belgium and Germany

31 DIVISION
Divisional Troops
223 Field Company Royal Engineers
5 January 1916 - 14 April 1919

WO95/2352/3

The Naval & Military Press Ltd
www.nmarchive.com
Published in association with The National Archives

Published by

The Naval & Military Press Ltd

Unit 10 Ridgewood Industrial Park,

Uckfield, East Sussex,

TN22 5QE England

Tel: +44 (0) 1825 749494

www.naval-military-press.com

www.nmarchive.com

This diary has been reprinted in facsimile from the original. Any imperfections are inevitably reproduced and the quality may fall short of modern type and cartographic standards.

© Crown Copyright
Images reproduced by permission of The National Archives, London, England, 2015.

Contents

Document type	Place/Title	Date From	Date To
Heading	WO95/2352/3		
Heading	31st Division Divl Engineers 23rd Field Coy R.E. Mar 1916-Apr 1919		
War Diary	Ras-El-Esh (From Port Said)	05/01/1916	05/01/1916
War Diary	Tineh From (Ras-El-Esh)	06/01/1916	06/01/1916
War Diary	El Cap	07/01/1916	07/01/1916
War Diary	Kantara	08/01/1916	09/01/1916
War Diary	Post 70	10/01/1916	29/01/1916
War Diary	HT Tlandouery Castle	03/03/1916	03/03/1916
War Diary	Hocquincourt	12/03/1916	23/03/1916
War Diary	Beauval	27/03/1916	27/03/1916
War Diary	Mailly-Maille	30/03/1916	30/03/1916
War Diary	Colincamps	06/04/1916	30/06/1916
Heading	War Diary Of 23rd Field Company. R.E. 1-7-16 To 31-7-16 Volume VII		
War Diary	Les Huits Maisons	18/07/1916	31/07/1916
War Diary	Colincamps	01/07/1916	05/07/1916
War Diary	Bus	06/07/1916	06/07/1916
War Diary	Gezaincourt	07/07/1916	07/07/1916
War Diary	Longuevillette	08/07/1916	09/07/1916
War Diary	Quentin	10/07/1916	15/07/1916
War Diary	Les Huits Maisons	16/07/1916	17/07/1916
Heading	War Diary Of 223rd Field Company R.E. From 1-8-16 To 31-8-16 Volume VIII		
War Diary	Les Huits Maisons	01/08/1916	31/08/1916
Heading	War Diary 223rd Field Coy R.E. 31st Division September 1916 Vol 7		
War Diary	Les 8 Maisons Sheet 36 A.S.E. 1/20,000 Ref. R. 29 B 3.8	01/09/1916	16/09/1916
War Diary	Le Touret 36 A.S.E. 1/20000 15 D 8.2	17/09/1916	30/09/1916
Heading	War Diary Of 223rd Field Coy. R.E. October 1916 Volume X		
War Diary	Bertrancourt (Tents)	17/10/1916	17/10/1916
War Diary	Courcelles (Billets)	18/10/1916	19/10/1916
War Diary	Coigneux	20/10/1916	31/10/1916
War Diary	Le Touret 36 A.S.E. 1/20000 X 15d. 8.2	01/10/1916	04/10/1916
War Diary	Robecq. P. 35.c. 2.7	05/10/1916	08/10/1916
War Diary	Sarton	09/10/1916	12/10/1916
War Diary	Bertrancourt	13/10/1916	16/10/1916
Heading	War Diary. 223rd Field Coy. R.E. 31st Division November 1916 Vol 9		
War Diary	Coigneux Huts at J 3.a.7.3	01/11/1916	30/11/1916
Heading	War Diary Of 223rd Field Company. R.E. From 1/12/16 To 31/12/16 Volume XII		
War Diary	Coigneux Huts J. 3.a. 7.3	01/12/1916	31/12/1916
Heading	War Diary Of 223rd Field Company R.E. From 1-1-17 To 31-1-17 Volume 13		
War Diary	Coigneux	01/01/1917	31/01/1917
Heading	War Diary Of 223rd Field Company R.E. From 1/2/17 To 28/2/17 Vol XIV		

War Diary	Coigneux	01/02/1917	05/02/1917
War Diary	Bernaville	06/02/1917	08/02/1917
War Diary	Bonneville	09/02/1917	19/02/1917
War Diary	Beauquesne	20/02/1917	20/02/1917
War Diary	J 3. C 5.9	21/02/1917	28/02/1917
Heading	War Diary Of Major J. Cochran R.E. 223rd Field Co. R.E. From 1st March 1917 To 31st March 1917 Inclusive Volume 15		
War Diary	J 3 C. 5.9	01/03/1917	04/03/1917
War Diary	Huts	05/03/1917	05/03/1917
War Diary	Coigneux	06/03/1917	18/03/1917
War Diary	Beauquesne	19/03/1917	19/03/1917
War Diary	Beauvoir	20/03/1917	20/03/1917
War Diary	Blangermont	21/03/1917	21/03/1917
War Diary	Faux	22/03/1917	23/03/1917
War Diary	Flechinelle	24/03/1917	24/03/1917
War Diary	St. Venant	25/03/1917	25/03/1917
War Diary	Berquette Rd Billets	26/03/1917	31/03/1917
Heading	War Diary Of 223rd Field Coy R.E. Apl 1st To Apl 30th 1917 Vol XVI		
War Diary	St. Venant Billets	01/04/1917	01/04/1917
War Diary	Berguette Rd	02/04/1917	02/04/1917
War Diary	Bethune Billets	03/04/1917	03/04/1917
War Diary	Gouy Servins Tents And Huts. R.E. Yard	04/04/1917	09/04/1917
War Diary	Under Canvas Near Lamotte Farm	11/04/1917	11/04/1917
War Diary	Mont St Eloy	12/04/1917	15/04/1917
War Diary	Ecoivres	16/04/1917	16/04/1917
War Diary	Hutments.	17/04/1917	21/04/1917
War Diary	Ecoivres.	22/04/1917	22/04/1917
War Diary	Hutments	29/04/1917	29/04/1917
War Diary	Bivouacs at 99 B 3.3. N. of St Nicholas.	30/04/1917	30/04/1917
Heading	War Diary Of 223rd Field Company R.E. From May 1st. 1917 To May 31st, 1917 Volume XVII		
War Diary	H.Q. Bivonacs at G. 9.b. 6.2	01/05/1917	19/05/1917
War Diary	Ecoivres	20/05/1917	20/05/1917
War Diary	Hutments	21/05/1917	31/05/1917
Heading	War Diary Of 223rd Field Company. R.E. From 1st June. 1917 To June 30th. 1917. Volume XVIII		
War Diary	Ecoivres.	01/06/1917	01/06/1917
War Diary	Hutments.	05/06/1917	09/06/1917
War Diary	G 9.d. 3.7	10/06/1917	30/06/1917
Heading	War Diary Of 223rd Field Company. R.E. July 1st To July 31st. 1917 Volume XIX		
War Diary	G.9.d. 3.7	01/07/1917	03/07/1917
War Diary	G. 10b 8.2	04/07/1917	31/07/1917
Heading	War Diary Of 223rd Field Company. R.E. From 1/8/17 To 31/8/17 Volume XX		
War Diary		01/08/1917	01/08/1917
War Diary	Aux. Rietz	02/08/1917	02/08/1917
War Diary	G.1.b. 8.2	05/08/1917	30/08/1917
Heading	War Diary Of 223rd Field Company. R.E. From 1/9/17 To 30/9/17 Volume XX		
War Diary	Aux. Rietz G. 10.b. 8.2	01/09/1917	06/09/1917
War Diary	A 18.b.8.6	06/09/1917	17/09/1917
War Diary	Ecurie	18/09/1917	18/09/1917
War Diary	A 27b. 8.3	19/09/1917	30/09/1917

Heading	War Diary Of 223rd Field Company. R.E. October 1st, 1917 To October 31st. 1917 Volume XXII		
War Diary	Ecurie A 27.b 8.3	01/10/1917	30/10/1917
Heading	War Diary Of 223rd Field Company. R.E. From 1/11/17 To 30/11/17 Volume XXIII		
War Diary	Ecurie A 27b. 8.3	01/11/1917	03/12/1917
Heading	War Diary Of 223rd Field Company R.E. 223rd Field Company. R.E. From 1/12/17 To 31/12/17 Volume XXIV		
War Diary	Ecurie A 27b. 8.3	02/12/1917	06/12/1917
War Diary	ACQ (Billets)	07/12/1917	20/12/1917
War Diary	Ecurie A 27b. 8.3	21/12/1917	31/12/1917
Heading	War Diary Of 223rd Field Company. R.E. 1/1/18 To 31/1/18 Volume XXV.		
War Diary	Ecurie A 27b. 8.3	01/01/1918	30/01/1918
Heading	War Diary Of 223rd Field Company. R.E. From 1/2/18 To 28/2/18 Volume XXVI		
War Diary	A 27.b. 8.3	01/02/1918	28/02/1918
Heading	31st Divisional Engineers. War Diary 223rd Field Company R.E. March 1918		
Heading	War Diary Of 223rd Field Company. R.E. From 1/3/18 To 31/3/18 Volume XXVII		
War Diary	Aubrey Camp A 28.a. 2.1	01/03/1918	21/03/1918
War Diary	Blaireville	22/03/1918	22/03/1918
War Diary	Courcelles les Comte	23/03/1918	24/03/1918
War Diary	Douchy Les Ayette	25/03/1918	25/03/1918
War Diary	Monchy An Bois	26/03/1918	27/03/1918
War Diary	Bienvillers	28/03/1918	30/03/1918
War Diary	Gaudiempre	31/03/1918	31/03/1918
Heading	31st Divisional Engineers 223rd Field Company R.E. April 1918		
War Diary	War Diary Of 223rd Field Company. R.E. 223rd Field Company. R.E. From 1/4/18 To 30/4/18 Volume XXVIII		
War Diary	Oppy Caucourt	01/04/1918	08/04/1918
War Diary	Kermin	09/04/1918	11/04/1918
War Diary	Merris	11/04/1918	13/04/1918
War Diary	Hondeghem	13/04/1918	18/04/1918
War Diary	Au Souverain	19/04/1918	26/04/1918
War Diary	Hutments V8. D34 Mile & of Hondeghem	27/04/1918	29/04/1918
Heading	War Diary Of 223rd Field Company. R.E. 223rd Field Company. R.E. From 1/5/18 To 31/5/18 Volume XXIX		
War Diary	Hutments V8 D 3.4 1/2 Mile 5 of Hondeghem	01/05/1918	20/05/1918
War Diary	Roukloshille R 31 D 4.1 Transport Lines. V 8 d 3.4	21/05/1918	22/05/1918
War Diary	Racquinghem	23/05/1918	31/05/1918
Heading	War Diary Of 223rd Field Company R.E. 223rd Field Company. R.E. From 1st June To 30th June, 1918 Volume XXX		
War Diary	Racquinghem	01/06/1918	15/06/1918
War Diary	Hondeghem	16/06/1918	17/06/1918
War Diary	Eek Hout Cassel	17/06/1918	20/06/1918
War Diary	Hazebrouck Garage	21/06/1918	23/06/1918
War Diary	D 96. 3.4	24/06/1918	24/06/1918
War Diary	D 9b 5.4. & of Hazebrouck	25/06/1918	30/06/1918
Heading	War Diary Of 223rd Field Company. R.E. From 1/7/18 To 31/7/18 Volume XXX		

War Diary	Sub Hazebrouck D.9.b.5.4	01/07/1918	30/07/1918
Heading	War Diary Of 223rd Field Company. R.E. From 1/8/18 To 31/8/18 Volume XXXII		
War Diary	S Of Hazebrouck D 9.b. 5.4	01/08/1918	22/08/1918
War Diary	W. Of Fletre W 4.d 4.4	23/08/1918	30/08/1918
War Diary	Les. Ormes W. of Meteren	31/08/1918	31/08/1918
Heading	War Diary Of 223rd Field Company. R.E. From 1st Sept. To 30th Sept. 1918 Volume XXXII		
War Diary	Les. Ormes W. of Meteren	01/09/1918	03/09/1918
War Diary	SE. Bailleul S.27.C.7.5	04/09/1918	27/09/1918
War Diary	T.30.b. 4.2 East Of Bailleul	28/09/1918	29/09/1918
War Diary	O. 14.a. 4.6 S Of Messines.	29/09/1918	30/09/1918
Heading	War Diary Of 223rd Field Company. R.E. From 1/10/18 To 31/10/18 Volume XXXIV		
War Diary	Adv. Camp At W 14.b. 5.8. Transport Lines At 16b. 2.8	01/10/1918	03/10/1918
War Diary	Hill. 6.3. W15a 5.9	04/10/1918	15/10/1918
War Diary	Hill 6.3. Nr Ploegsteert	16/10/1918	16/10/1918
War Diary	Hill 6.3	17/10/1918	17/10/1918
War Diary	Warneton	18/10/1918	18/10/1918
War Diary	Rubaix Filature Du Nord	19/10/1918	19/10/1918
War Diary	Rubaix on Banks of the Canal de Rubaix.	20/10/1918	20/10/1918
War Diary	Lannoy Rue. Du. Bois.	21/10/1918	21/10/1918
War Diary	Nechin	22/10/1918	22/10/1918
War Diary	Pecq	23/10/1918	23/10/1918
War Diary	Nechin	24/10/1918	25/10/1918
War Diary	Mouscron	26/10/1918	27/10/1918
War Diary	Staceghem	28/10/1918	31/10/1918
Heading	War Diary Of 223rd Field Company. R.E. From 1/11/18 To 30/11/18 Volume XXXV		
War Diary	Staceghem	01/11/1918	02/11/1918
War Diary	Halluin	03/11/1918	06/11/1918
War Diary	Staceghem	07/11/1918	08/11/1918
War Diary	Ooteghem Rugge.	09/11/1918	09/11/1918
War Diary	Rugge	10/11/1918	10/11/1918
War Diary	Ruyen	11/11/1918	12/11/1918
War Diary	Avelghem	14/11/1918	14/11/1918
War Diary	Lauwe	15/11/1918	22/11/1918
War Diary	Menin	23/11/1918	23/11/1918
War Diary	Ypres	24/11/1918	24/11/1918
War Diary	Steenvorde	25/11/1918	25/11/1918
War Diary	Arques	26/11/1918	30/11/1918
Heading	War Diary Of 223rd Field Company. R.E. From 1/12/18 To 31/12/18 Volume XXXVI		
War Diary	Arques	01/12/1918	31/12/1918
Heading	War Diary Of The 223rd. Field Company R.E. For The Month Of January, 1919. Volume 37		
War Diary	Arques.	01/01/1919	01/01/1919
War Diary	Stomer	03/01/1919	31/01/1919
Heading	War Diary 223rd Field Company, Royal Engineers. February, 1919		
War Diary	Stomer	01/02/1919	14/04/1919

WO95/
2352(3)

31ST DIVISION
DIVL ENGINEERS

223RD FIELD COY R.E.

MAR ~~JAN~~ 1916 - APR 1919

Instructions regarding War Diaries and Intelligence Summaries are contained in F. S. Regs., Part II. and the Staff Manual respectively. Title Pages will be prepared in manuscript.

Jan '16
Apr 19

WAR DIARY or INTELLIGENCE SUMMARY of 223rd Field Coy R.E.

(Erase heading not required.)

XXXI

Army Form C. 2118

Vol 1 & 2

Place	Date	Hour	Summary of Events and Information	Remarks and references to Appendices
RAS-EL-ESH (from Port Said)	5-1-16	8.15 PM.	With the object of reconnoitring and clearing a road for wheeled transport along the Western bank of the SUEZ Canal the dismounted portion of Company marched out of Camp at PORT SAID 8.45 a.m with 1 double G.S. wagon (¾ load) and 4 pack cobs carrying tools. 1 section employed in removing obstacles on track. Reached RAS-EL-ESH 2 p.m. Storm and rain in evening. Bivouacked (mostly under buildings). Remainder of animals and drivers moved part under Capt Walker by train to KANTARA part remained with remainder of vehicles in camp under Lt Cochran at PORT SAID. 1 Platoon 12th Y & L in occupation of RAS-EL-ESH.	
TINEH (from RAS-EL-ESH 6¼ m)	6-1-16	5.0 pm	Marched from RAS-EL-ESH 8.15 a.m. arrived TINEH 12.30 p.m. Found Head Quarters of a Company of 12th Y & L in occupation. Very heavy going after rain overnight. Cyclists obliged to cycle by the side of the railway line. Worst portions about ¾ mile south of RAS-EL-ESH for ¼ mile dredged material had been deposited on the bank.	
EL CAP (6 m)	7-1-6.	5.0 PM	Marched from TINEH 8.15 a.m. Arrived EL CAP 11.20 AM. One Company 15th West Yorks in occupation. Weather very cool. Heavy going over first mile remainder good. No obstruction other than firing trenches across the track ¾ km North of EL CAP and inside EL CAP post. Cyclists rode along Railway. Bivouacked in a wood West of railway line.	
KANTARA (6 m)	8-1-6	3.15 PM	Marched from EL CAP 8.45 a.m ~~2 halts of 10 and 20 minutes~~ arrived in camp at KANTARA 12.30 PM. Delayed through filling in trenches across the road for passage of G.S. wagon and 1½ hours in ferrying across the SUEZ CANAL. Route followed was that West of the Sweetwater Canal and was very rugged in places the holes from which telegraph poles had recently been removed were only half filled in and careful driving was necessary to avoid them.	
ditto	9-1-6		Company rested at KANTARA. O.C. rode in to POST 70 to make arrangements with O.C. of that post to move there. 2nd Lt Jackson 12 Drivers and 24 animals arrived at KANTARA by train. 2nd Lt Jackson taken into hospital.	
POST 70	10-1-6	3.20 PM	Marched from KANTARA 9.0 AM. arrived in camp at POST 70 12.30 PM	3 sappers 11.20 R marched into POST 70.

1875 Wt. W593/826 1,000,000 4/15 J.B.C. & A. A.D.S.S./Forms/C. 2118.

Instructions regarding War Diaries and Intelligence Summaries are contained in F. S. Regs., Part II. and the Staff Manual respectively. Title Pages will be prepared in manuscript.

WAR DIARY of 223rd Field Coy R.E.
or
~~INTELLIGENCE SUMMARY~~
(Erase heading not required.)

Army Form C. 2118

(2)

Place	Date	Hour	Summary of Events and Information	Remarks and references to Appendices
POST 70	13·1·16	8·30 PM	Working parties daily 11th 12th & 13th on firing and support trenches of position. Greatly handicapped by shortage of material. C.R.E. visited from KANTARA forenoon of 11th.	
POST 70	29·1·16	9·0 PM	G.O.C. visited front line trenches on 22·1·16 and ordered all work to be stopped owing to incorrect siting on right flank. Col Grant and C.R.E. arrived on 24·1·16, rode along front line and passed the greater part of the sites. These two officers selected reserve positions on left flank on afternoon of 25th (Bad weather prevented any work in the morning) and marked out a portion of the HILL 80 position on the morning of the 26th returning direct to KANTARA the same afternoon. Digging was resumed on the HILL 70 position on the 26th and on HILL 80 position on the 28th. Work continued satisfactorily over the 29th. 2nd Lt Jackson rejoined from sick leave 27·1·16. Moved No 1 section under Lt Swales to Hill 80.	
HT Llandovery Castle	3·3·16	6·15 PM	Moved No 2 section under Lt Cochran to HILL 80 on 8/2/16. Moved 1 N.C.O & 5 men (No 3 section) to EL OUEIDAR to improve wells and 1 N.C.O & 5 men (No 4 section) for similar work at EL NUSS on 25·2·16. 1 N.C.O 19 Drivers 21 animals transferred to 13th Division on 14·2·16. Captn Walker with 23 mounted N.C.O^s and men left as advance party to embark at Port Said on 29·2·16. Moved 4 sections from HILLS 70 & 80 to KANTARA on afternoon of 27·2·16. Transferred remaining horses and mules and all vehicles and harness to 1/2 Lowland Field Coy at KANTARA on 1/3/16. On same night 4 mounted men and 8 Officers chargers left by train for ALEXANDRIA and remainder of Company viz 5 Officers 177 O.R. entrained for PORT SAID embarking on the forenoon of 2·3·16.	
HOCQUINCOURT	12·3·16	6·15 PM	Arrived MARSEILLES early morning of 8·3·16. Disembarked 7·0 p.m. entrained 11·30 p.m. Detrained at PONT REMY midnight of 10th & 11th. marched to HOCQUINCOURT and put the men into billets. rearranged billets in forenoon of 11·3·16.	
"	23·3·16	10·30 PM	Since last entry Company was practised in marching and marking out trench lines by night taking precautions against bombing from aeroplanes and gas attacks. Orders for march received on 22·3·16. Motored with Captn Miller to see C.R.E. 36th Division re taking over. Visited billets of Field Coys at MAILLY-MAILLET and ENGELBELMER. Lt Swales & 4 N.C.O^s sent to 48th Division for instruction in trench work 22·3·16.	

1875 Wt. W593/826 1,000,000 4/15 J.B.C. & A. A.D.S.S./Forms/C. 2118.

Instructions regarding War Diaries and Intelligence Summaries are contained in F. S. Regs., Part II. and the Staff Manual respectively. Title Pages will be prepared in manuscript.

WAR DIARY of 223rd Field Coy RE
or
~~INTELLIGENCE SUMMARY~~
(Erase heading not required.)

Army Form C. 2118

(3)

Place	Date	Hour	Summary of Events and Information	Remarks and references to Appendices
BEAUVAL	27-3-16	4.0 PM	25/3/16 Left HOCQUINCOURT 9 a.m. marched via HALLENCOURT WANEL to LONGPRÉ 12-30 billeted 26/3/16 Left LONGPRÉ 8-10 a.m. marched with 93rd Inf Bde via CONDÉ, HANGEST, BOURDON, PT 77, VIGNACOURT to FLESSELLES 3-30 p.m. billeted. Lt Swales & 4 NCOs rejoined 27/3/16 Left FLESSELLES 9 a.m. marched via NAOURS. VERTGALAND FARM to BEAUVAL 1.0 PM billeted	25/3/16 5 O 215 OR billeted 27/3/16 6 O 219 OR billeted
MAILLY-MAILLET	30-3-16	8-45 AM	28/3/16 Left BEAUVAL 10-30 a.m. marched via BEAUQUESNE MARIEUX LOUVENCOURT, BERTRANCOURT (halted till dusk) BEAUSSART to MAILLY MAILLET (8-30 p.m.) billeted. 29/3/16 One working party from each section working at tram line & dugouts at night.	
COLINCAMPS	6-4-16	9.0 PM	2/4/16 Lt Swales & No 1 section moved to billets in COLINCAMPS Lt Cochran & No 2 section to COURCELLES 3/4/16 Handed over SERRE ROAD to REDAN front to West Riding Coy RE and took over WATLING STREET to LUKE COPSE front from 2/1st So Midland Co RE 4/4/16 4-6 Company employed in opening up old & new communication trenches & main avenues. Heavy Artillery fire on both sides on the night of the 6th	
COLINCAMPS	30-4-16	10 PM	Company employed since last entry on Bde H.Q. dug outs new communication trenches, clearing and repairing front and support lines and main avenues water supply to trenches and administrative work in COLINCAMPS. L/c Cpl Longfield killed 24.4.16 by rifle grenade while taking a party to work in front line. Work done under difficulties owing to heavy rain which was almost continuous up to 25-4-16. Night working parties had some difficulty in completing new communication trenches owing to fire of machine guns which the enemy appeared to lay on any new work noticed during the day ready for the resumption of work at night. Lieut Jackson taken to hospital on 19-4-16 and Capt Walker summoned to England on 28-4-16 on urgent private affairs left the Unit handicapped through shortage of officers	Present 4 Offrs 200 OR.

G. H. Goodman [?] Major RE
O.C. 223. F.C. RE.
1.5.16.

1875 Wt. W593/826 1,000,000 4/15 J.B.C. & A. A.D.S.S./Forms/C. 2118.

Instructions regarding War Diaries and Intelligence Summaries are contained in F. S. Regs., Part II. and the Staff Manual respectively. Title Pages will be prepared in manuscript.

WAR DIARY
or
~~INTELLIGENCE SUMMARY~~
(Erase heading not required.)

~~81~~ Mayo June 223 Co R.E. Vol. 3·4.

Army Form C. 2118

Place	Date	Hour	Summary of Events and Information	Remarks and references to Appendices
COLINCAMPS	7.5.16.		Lieut Swales to Hospital and evacuated to England and replaced by 2nd Lieut Keating on 13.5.16	
	10.5.16.		Lieut KEATING joined for duty.	
"	22.5/16		Major Goodwin wounded by a shell near the front line and evacuated to Hospital. Sergt Hammond died of wounds and Cpl Whitehead wounded.	
	25.5/16		Lieut Cox joined for duty	
	28.5/16		Captain R.E. Dewing joined from 21st Division to command the Company.	
			The Company employed on making a new support line and opening up communication trenches. Work interrupted by enemy artillery on several occasions. A few wet days also hindered the work. Working parties were generally under strength.	
	7/6.		Two wet days considerably hinder work in Trenches. No2 Section digging dugouts for the Company. No4 at Div R.E. Park. No1 & 3 in Trenches.	
	8/6/16		Wet weather continued. No1 Sec working on assembly trenches & ration dumps. No2 Sec. on dugouts back at Colincamps. No3 Sec. on deep dugouts in trenches. No4 Sec on R.E dump Courcelles.	
	10/6/16		Lt Keating was wounded in left arm (rifle bullet) whilst reconnoitring support line (proposed).	
	12/6/16		Received notice Lt Keating had been evacuated. Wet weather	
	30/6/16		still continued hindering work considerably. Same class of work continued. viz Ration dumps. dugouts. trench bridges. clearing communication trenches & assembly ditto. G.K. [illegible] Capt R.E. for O.C. 223 Coy R.E.	

1875 Wt. W593/826 1,000,000 4/15 J.B.C. & A. A.D.S.S./Forms/C. 2118.

WO 95/2947

CONFIDENTIAL

WAR DIARY

OF

223RD FIELD COMPANY. R.E

1-7-16 TO 31-7-16

Volume VII

Army Form C. 2118

WAR DIARY
or
~~INTELLIGENCE SUMMARY~~
(Erase heading not required.)

Instructions regarding War Diaries and Intelligence Summaries are contained in F. S. Regs., Part II. and the Staff Manual respectively. Title Pages will be prepared in manuscript.

223rd Fd Coy RE
July 1916

~~Place~~ Date	Date	Hour	Summary of Events and Information	Remarks and references to Appendices
18/7/16.	Les HUITS MAISONS		Ordered to have 2 parties of 20 men & 2 officers ready to accompany raiding parties of 92nd Bde to consolidate captured trenches. This order was cancelled at 9 pm. Party working at Bomb Store & Bombing Ground for 94th Bde, party at water supply at VIEILLE CHAPELLE.	HL
19/7/16			Parties working as above. No 1 Section start 3 dugouts for "IT" in Grants Post	HL
20/7/16			Arranged for Lt COCHRAN & No 3 Sect. to open Trench School for ~~No~~ 93rd Bde (7 days)	HL
21/7/16.		"	Parties working at Fd Ambulance at VIEILLE CHAPELLE, repairs to water supply & improvements to Hospital. Ration dumps for Dvn ASC. Bomb stores for 93rd Bde.	HL
22/7/16		"	" " "	HL
23/7/16			"	HL
24/7/16			" "	HL
25/7/16.			As above Trench School closed as 93rd Bde went into trenches	HL
26/7/16			Parties as above. In shops making sample dugouts & making sample trenches in Billets.	HL
27/7/16			Parties as above Lt MOORE went to WIMEREUX to attend course in construction of Arty O.P.s	HL
28/7/16.			Parties as above.	HL
29/7/16.			Parties as above	HL
30/7/16			Lt COX & No 4 section commenced work on Bomb stores for T.M. in RUE de BOIS, also work on CHURCH Redoubt	HL
31/7/16.			Parties as above, started Instructional School for 94th Infy Bde under Lt C[illegible]	HL

[illegible] Major RE
Cmdg 223rd [illegible]

1875 Wt. W593/826 1,000,000 4/15 J.B.C. & A. A.D.S.S./Forms/C. 2118.

Instructions regarding War Diaries and Intelligence Summaries are contained in F. S. Regs., Part II. and the Staff Manual respectively. Title Pages will be prepared in manuscript.

WAR DIARY
or
~~INTELLIGENCE SUMMARY~~
(Erase heading not required.)

Army Form C. 2118

223 Coy R.E. (5)
July 1916

Place	Date	Hour	Summary of Events and Information	Remarks and references to Appendices
COLINCAMPS	1/7/16		Attack started 7.30 am. preceded by intense bombardment.	FC
"	2/7/16		Received orders to repair trenches. 3 Sections proceed to work on Comm^n trenches by day 1 Sect. worked by night. 2 Casualties (slightly wounded).	FC
"	3/7/16		2 Sections worked on Communications to Front line by day, 2 Sections by night	FC
"	4/7/16		" " " + Front Line, " "	FC
"	5/7/16		Marched from COLINCAMPS at 8 a.m. whole company in BUS that night	FC
BUS	6/7/16		" " BUS with 94th Bde at 8.30 a.m. arrived at GEZAINCOURT at 3 P.M.	FC
GEZAINCOURT	7/7/16		" " GEZAINCOURT at 2 P.M. to billets at LONGUEVILETTE arriving at 2.45 pm	FC
LONGUEVILLETTE	8/7/16		" " LONGUEVILETTE at 9 P.M. arrived at FREVENT at 2.30 am	FC
	9/7/16		Entrained at FREVENT at 6.37 a.m. Detrained at STEENBECQUE at 10 a.m.	
QUENTIN			Marched to Billets at QUENTIN near CALONNE arriving at 3.30 p.m.	FC
"	10/7/16 to 13/7/16		In billets at QUENTIN, resting + cleaning up – Drill + Field works	FC
"	14/7/16		At QUENTIN under orders to move billets on Div^n taking up line Near NEUVE CHAPELLE	FC
	15/7/16		Marched at 12 noon to billets in LES 8 MAISONS near FOSSE arriving 2.30 pm	FC
LES HUITS MAISONS	16/7/16		Men have hot baths + take over R.E. dumps in billets + at RICHEBOURG ST VAAST	FC
	17/7/16		Cleaning up billets + reconnoitring new line	FC

F J Collins Capt R.E. O.C. 223 Fd Co

1875 Wt. W593/826 1,000,000 4/15 J.B.C. & A. A.D.S.S./Forms/C. 2118.

ORIGINAL

Confidential

War Diary

of

223rd Field Company R.E.

from 1-8-16 to 31-8-16

VOLUME VIII

Instructions regarding War Diaries and Intelligence Summaries are contained in F. S. Regs., Part II. and the Staff Manual respectively. Title Pages will be prepared in manuscript.

WAR DIARY or ~~INTELLIGENCE SUMMARY~~

(Erase heading not required.)

Army Form C. 2118

Vol 7. August 1916.

Place	Date	Hour	Summary of Events and Information	Remarks and references to Appendices
LES HUITS MAISONS	1-8-16		Company working in the back area. Employed on Arty O.P.S. Dugouts for Trench Mortars R.A.M.C. Bde Bomb Stores. Moving Huts – water supply. Repairs etc. Also instructional school in Trench Engineering for Bde in Div[l] Reserve	HC
"	2-8-16 to 7-8-16		do do do	HC
"	8-8-16		Company working in back area. Employed on Art[y] O.Ps Dugouts for RAMC Bomb stores. Moving huts for D.A.C. Hospital Floors & repairs at VIEILLE CHAPELLE. Instructional School for Bde in Reserve at R.19.d.2.0 & huts for Div[l] School at PACAUT. No 2 Sect. proceeded to PACAUT & be billeted there on 8.8.16. to huts above huts	HC
"	9-8-16		do do	HC
"	10-8-16		Company employed as above. Lt COUTTAS & No 1 Sect with Thistle wagon to billets in LE TOURET & work in trenches in 93rd Bde area (QUINQUE RUE – GRENADIER trench. 92nd Bde on the left, 30th Div[n] on right. Work – fire steps in RICHMOND TERRACE. Opening support line from RICHMOND TERRACE to ROPE TRENCH. Revetting SHETLAND AV. with U-frames & hurdles.	HC
"	11-8-16 12		Company Employed. No 2 Section. Div[l] School PACAUT Huts etc. No 1 Sect. Trenches in FESTUBERT sector with 93rd Bde. No 3 Sect. Art[y] O.Ps etc. No 4 Section Concrete floors at VIEILLE CHAPELLE, more old trenches at ZELOBES & alteration to D.A.C. Amm[n] Dumps.	HC
"	13.8.16		Company employed as above. Lt Cox left for month's course at 1st Army School	HC
"	14.8.16 15.8.16		do do do	HC

F. Collins Capt R.E.
O.C. 223rd (Field) Coy. R.E.

Instructions regarding War Diaries and Intelligence Summaries are contained in F. S. Regs., Part II. and the Staff Manual respectively. Title Pages will be prepared in manuscript.

WAR DIARY
or
INTELLIGENCE SUMMARY
(Erase heading not required.)

Army Form C. 2118

Vol 7 (cont^d) August 1916

Place	Date	Hour	Summary of Events and Information	Remarks and references to Appendices
LES HUIT MAISONS	16.8.16		Company employed as follows — billets at LETOURET. No 1 Sect with Lt COULTAS in trenches in FESTUBERT sector with 93rd Bde No 2 Sect Building huts + constructing F.E. course for Div^{nl} School + billets at PACAUT. No 3 Sect Arty O.P.S + gun pits + S.A.A Stores in Div^{nl} Area. No 4 Sect Concrete floors for RAMC at VIEILLE CHAPELLE, for ASC in Supply Dumps Model trenches at ZELOBES + LA C^{ce} MARMUSE.	[initialled]
"	17.8.16			[initialled]
"	18.8.16		Lt COULTAS + No 1 Section handed over work in FESTUBERT sector to O.C. 201 F^d Coy R.E. 30th Div + returned to billets at 6 p.m. here. Remainder work as above.	[initialled]
"	19.8.16		Work as above. No 1 Section work on Winter Horse standings in billets	[initialled]
"	20.8.16		No work except for No 2 Sect + Night work on O.Ps — Sunday	[initialled]
"	21.8.16		No 1 Section A.S.C concrete floors at FOSSE + ZELOBES, Bat^n H.Q. at PONT LOGY No 2 Section Building huts + bayonet fighting course at PACAUT, + facsimile of BOARS HEAD (German trench) at LA C^{ce} MARMUSE. Inst^{n} classes for 94th Bde + Div^{nl} School. No 3 Sect. Arty O.P.S, ladders + gun pits in Div^{nl} Area No 4 Sect. Work at VIEILLE CHAPELLE + model trenches at ZELOBES	[initialled]
↓			" " "	
"	26.8.16		" "	[initialled]
"	27.8.16		Work as above, Inst Classes for Div^{nl} school only at PACAUT	
"	29.8.16		No 4 Section Concrete floors for A.S.C dumps at ZELOBES + LOCON + bridge ... at FOSSE	[initialled]
"	30.8.16 }		Work as above No 3 Section finished at PACAUT and commenced RAMC dugouts at	
"	31.8.16 }		Green barn + LANSDOWNE House (Bat^n H.Q	[initialled]

F Collin Capt R.E.
O.C. 223rd (Field) Coy. R.E.

1875 Wt. W593/826 1,000,000 4/15 J.B.C. & A. A.D.S.S./Forms/C. 2118.

Confidential   Vol ~~III~~ 7

War Diary

223rd Field Coy R.E.   31st Division

September 1916.

Instructions regarding War Diaries and Intelligence Summaries are contained in F. S. Regs., Part II. and the Staff Manual respectively. Title Pages will be prepared in manuscript.

WAR DIARY
or
~~INTELLIGENCE SUMMARY~~
(Erase heading not required.)

Army Form C. 2118

Vol 8. Sept. 1916.

Place	Date	Hour	Summary of Events and Information	Remarks and references to Appendices
LES 8 MAISONS Sheet 36A.S.E 1/20000 Ref. R29b 3.8.	1.9.16		Company employed on works in back area of 31st Divn. No 1 Sect. Batn HQ Dugouts Etc at PONT LOGY, 2" T.M. Emplacement in front line at the NEB. No 3 Sect. Arty O.Ps (Chimney, Ladder etc) Gun pits in B Line. No 2 Section. Instn School for Officers & N.C.Os of 93rd & 94th Bde at R 35 d 2.9. RAMC Dugouts at Green barn & LANSDOWNE HOUSE Batn HQ. No 4 Section Model trenches at ZELOBES, repairs in VIEILLE CHAPELLE, RICHEBOURG etc.	HC
	7.9.16		do.	HC
"	8.9.16		No 1 Section finished Batn HQ at PONT LOGY & commenced work on gun pit in B line, T.M. Empt in front line. No 2 Sect Instn School for officers & N.C.Os of 93rd & 94th Bde at R 35 d 2.9 RAMC dugout at Greenbarn & Lansdowne House Batn HQ Capt Walker took Instn School at PACAUT in M.E. No 3 Sect. Arty O.Ps & gun pits in B Line. No 4 Section Model trenches at Zelobes Baths at RICHEBOURG. repairs at VIEILLE CHAPELLE etc.	HC
	16.9.16			
LETOURET. 36A S.E 1/20000 X 15 d 8.2	17.9.16 18.9.16		Marched at 9.30 a.m. on 17th & took over billets from 201st Fd Coy R.E. (30th Divn) at LETOURET, officers then reconnoitred FESTUBERT SECTOR	HC
	19.9.16		Commenced work in FESTUBERT sector with 94th Bde. No 1 Section. Front area from QUINQUE RUE - Island 14 - No 2 Section Front area from 13 a Island - Princes Island & New Cut. No 3 Section RA O.P.S & village line No 4 Section O.B.L & back work. 1 Coy XI Corps Cyclists attached for work working with No 1 & No 2 Sections. 'D' Coy 12th KOYLI attached for work working in SHETLAND, PIONEER, BARNTON LOOP CT.	HC
	23.9.16			
	24.9.16		Sunday - Rest - L/Cpl Dixter killed (bullet wound) on night work between Islands 30A & 30B	HC

Instructions regarding War Diaries and Intelligence Summaries are contained in F. S. Regs., Part II. and the Staff Manual respectively. Title Pages will be prepared in manuscript.

WAR DIARY
or
~~INTELLIGENCE SUMMARY~~
(Erase heading not required.)

Army Form C. 2118

Vol 8 (Contd) Sept 1916

Place	Date	Hour	Summary of Events and Information	Remarks and references to Appendices
LETOURET 36A SE/2000 X15d 82.	25/9/16 ↓ 30.9.16		No 1 Section joining Islands 16–20 Comm Trench (revetment foot boards, dugouts etc. (35 Cyclists attached) XI Corps Cyclists.	
			No 2 Section work on Princes Island. Revetting parapet, parados etc. New cut, reclaiming old sand bag breastwork (35 Cyclist attached)	
			No 3 Sect R.A. O.Ps in FESTUBERT & LE PLANTIN, dugouts on O.B.L, empl. for 4.T.M. near BARNTON.TEE. etc.	
			No 4. Back work, shops in billets, preparation for Demonstration of making trenches by tubes of Ammonal.	
			200 Infy (94th Infy Bde) working party at various places, & 100 Infy carrying party nightly from 26-9-16 – 30-9-16 according to scheme attached.	FC
			Line very quiet as both we & the enemy have a great deal of work to do – the FESTUBERT Sector is in a shocking condition, apparently no work has been done on the Islands since Oct '15 or they would not be Islands still; as this company has joined up about 80–100 yds in 8 days work – only employing parts of 2 sections on this work.	FC
			Warned to be ready to move to IV Army, in consequence all new work has been stopped. During the last week a working party of 200 Infy has been employed nightly on heightening & thickening parapets & filling in behind hurdles erected by this Coy also a carrying party of 100 nightly.	FC

F. Collier Capt RE
O.C. 223rd Fd Coy RE
30-9-16.

1875 Wt. W593/826 1,000,000 4/15 J.B.C. & A. A.D.S.S./Forms/C. 2118.

Confidential.

Vol 8

War Diary

of

223rd Field Coy: R.E.

October 1916

Volume X

Army Form C. 2118

Instructions regarding War Diaries and Intelligence Summaries are contained in F. S. Regs., Part II. and the Staff Manual respectively. Title Pages will be prepared in manuscript.

WAR DIARY
or
~~INTELLIGENCE SUMMARY~~

(Erase heading not required.)

223rd Fd Coy R.E. (31st Divn)
Vol 10 Oct 1916 (Contd)

Place	Date	Hour	Summary of Events and Information	Remarks and references to Appendices
BERTRAN (Tents) COURT	17-10-16	–	Carried on work on Divnl & Bde Battle H.Q.s	HC
COURCELLES (billets)	18-10-16		Moved into billets in C. at 11 am taking over billets & R.E. Yard from 1/2nd H. Fd Coy RE work as previously.	HC
"	19-10-16		Work as before.	
COIGNEUX.	20-10-16		Received orders at 12 noon to leave one section at COURCELLES & remainder to move to share billets at COIGNEUX. Lt. Cox & No 4 Section remained at COURCELLES	HC HC
"	21-10-16		Received orders to prepare for offensive. Lt. Cox evacuated to hospital & later to base. Lt Coulter takes over No 4 Sect. at Courcelles & carries on work of filling forward Dumps with RE Stores. The remaining sections employed on Corps O.P. – Revetting & levelling parapets for track for Tanks 2 Camouflage tank pits. Boarding floors of deep dugouts in PAPIN for 92nd Bde Battle H.Q. Relaying trench boards & laying more in newly dug trenches. Laying 1200 yds of Decauville tramway. Erecting Name boards for Trenches etc.	
" Huts at J3a 7.3	24-10-16			HC
"	25-10-16		Work as above, one section erecting steel shelters, Armstrong Huts & starting 2 shafts for deep dugouts for Divnl Battle H.Q. near COIGNEUX J9b 8.4	HC
"	26-10-16		Lt PORE arrived for duty, takes over No 4 Section at COURCELLES Lt Coulter returns to H.Q. & No 1 Section goes to tents in WARNIMONT WOODS to repair huts. Remainder of Coy employed in up keep of C.T.s behind Line CABER–BRISOUX–CARENTY–HOPE ST. Weather very bad & trenches got into bad condition.	HC
	31-10-16		Work as above. A working party of 250 of 1st Ind. Cav. Divn arrive & start work on saps in PAPIN	HC

F. J. Collins Capt. R.E.

1875 Wt. W593/826 1,000,000 4/15 J.B.C. & A. A.D.S.S./Forms/C. 2118.

Instructions regarding War Diaries and Intelligence Summaries are contained in F. S. Regs., Part II. and the Staff Manual respectively. Title Pages will be prepared in manuscript.

WAR DIARY
or
INTELLIGENCE SUMMARY

(Erase heading not required.)

223rd Fd Coy R.E. (31st Divn)

Vol 10. Oct. 1916

Army Form C. 2118

Place	Date	Hour	Summary of Events and Information	Remarks and references to Appendices
LETOURET 36A S.E. 1/20000	1.10.16		Sunday Rest except for marching order parade for inspection of Kits, Amn Boots Iron Ration etc	HL
X15d. 8.2	2.10.16	..	Most of the company in billets small parties went to trenches to finish works in hand. Lt Coultas & No1 Section erected canvas screen between Islands 23 & 22 without casualties in 40 mins	HL
	3.10.16		Handed over maps plans etc to O.C. 59th Fd Coy R.E. 5th Divn Route march 2 p.m.	HL
	4.10.16		Officers went round trenches with Officers of 59th Fd Coy R.E. Drill, fatigues & route march	HL
Robecq. P35 C2.7	5.10.16		Marched at 9.30 a.m. to new billets near ROBECQ P.35.C.2.7.	HL
	6.10.16 7		In billets, practice strong points, bivouacs knotting & lashing - Drills.	HL
	8.10.16		Marched at 4 p.m. to entrain at BERGUETTE at 6.40 p.m.,	HL
SARTON	9.10.16		Detrained at DOULLENS at 5.30 a.m., marched to SARTON to billet in 94th Bde area	HL
"	10.10.16		Rest & drills.	
"	11.10.16		Lt. MOORE & No 3 Section marched to Bivouacs near COLINCAMPS to work on trench tramway under C.R.E. 51st Divn	HL
..	12.10.16		Lt. COX & BUCHANAN & Nos 2 & 4 Sections marched to tent camp near BERTRANCOURT to commence work with 1 Coy KOYLI on Divn & 94th Bde Advd Battle HQ, west of COURCELLES	HL
BERTRANCOURT	13.10.16		HQrs & wagon lines marched at 9.30 a.m. to same camp as No 2 & 4 Sections. Lt Coultas & No 1 Sectn joined Lt MOORE in bivouacs near COLINCAMPS. Day & Night shifts continued on Divnl & Bde Battle HQ. with 4 shifts of 30 each of KOYLI	HL
"	14.10.16 15.10.16	}	Work as above	HL
"	16.10.16		Lt MOORE & COULTAS & 1 & 3 Sections rejoined HQrs received warning to move to COURCELLES	HL

F. H. Collins Capt R.E.
O.C. 223rd Fd Coy R.E.

1875 Wt. W593/826 1,000,000 4/15 J.B.C. & A. A.D.S.S./Forms/C. 2118.

Confidential

Volume XI

Vol 9

War Diary

223rd Field Coy. R.E.

31st Division

November 1916

Instructions regarding War Diaries and Intelligence Summaries are contained in F. S. Regs., Part II. and the Staff Manual respectively. Title Pages will be prepared in manuscript.

WAR DIARY
or
~~INTELLIGENCE SUMMARY~~
(Erase heading not required.)

223rd Fd Coy RE.

Vol. II.

Army Form C. 2118

Place	Date	Hour	Summary of Events and Information	Remarks and references to Appendices
COIGNEUX Huts at J3a.7.3	1.11.16		Lt Buchanan + No 2 Section to billets in COURCELLES to relieve Lt POPE + No 4 Section + work in HOME + NAIRNE Tr. upkeep for offensive. Lt Coutlaos i/c repairs to huts in WARNIMONT woods No 1 Section in tents there for work. Remainder work on trenches behind line CABER BRISOUX in upkeep + repairs for offensive.	FC
"	2.11.16		Work as above Lt POPE transferred to 133 A.T. Coy RE Lt BENNETT joins for duty.	FC
	↑ ↓ 5.11.16		Work as above	FC
"	6.11.16		Rest men have baths. (Lt Cochran left on special leave for home FWM)	FC
"	7.11.16 ↕ 9.11.16		Coy work on all lateral trenches behind BRISSOUX + on PAPIN + C.T.s behind it with Native Cav. New Bde H.Q. started at J17b5.5.	FC
	10.11.16		Work as above. Party start on NISSEN huts for 1 batn at J.19.d.8.7	FC
	11.11.16		Work on C.T's. for forward operations. Working party of Native Cavalry left this morning. Capt. F. S. Collins left company on attachment to G.S. 31st Divn + handed over to Lt F W. Moore. Nissen Hutments continued.	FWM
	12.11.16		Work on C.T's + refilling the forward Dumps of R.E materials. Nissen Huts continued. Bde. H.Q finished.	FWM
	13.11.16		Forward operations by Divn. Nos. 2 + 4 sections kept in to relieve 211th Coy. if called on, but were not required. 12 men (volunteers) in line for making Bangalore trench connection to German lines but were also not called on. Other work on Nissen Huts continued	FWM
	14.11.16 ↕ 17.11.16		Normal work again restored and work of clearing C.T's after operations proceeded with. Work on YELLOW LINE continued and also the Nissen Hutments + Coy. Horse Standings. No. 1. Section relieved No. 2 at COURCELLES and No. 2. relieved No. 1. on NISSEN Huts.	FWM
	18.11.16		Work on YELLOW LINE continued, also Nissen Hutments + Horse standings. Lt. P. Cochran returned from special leave + took over the command of the Coy from Lt. F W MOORE.	FWM.
	19.11.16		Work on YELLOW LINE continued also NISSEN Hutments + Horse Standings.	P.C
	20.11.16		Work on YELLOW LINE continued also NISSEN Hutments + horse standings. Wiring YELLOW LINE commenced Section I moved from COURCELLES to THE DELL.	
	21.11.16		Work ditto. Section 4 moved from COIGNEUX to THE DELL.	P.C

1875 Wt. W593/826 1,000,000 4/15 J.B.C. & A. A.D.S.S./Forms/C. 2118.

Instructions regarding War Diaries and Intelligence Summaries are contained in F. S. Regs., Part II. and the Staff Manual respectively. Title Pages will be prepared in manuscript.

WAR DIARY
or
INTELLIGENCE SUMMARY
(Erase heading not required.)

223rd Field Co R E
Vol 11 (Continued)

Army Form C. 2118

Place	Date	Hour	Summary of Events and Information	Remarks and references to Appendices
COIGNEUX Huts at J.3 a.7.3	22.11.16		Work on YELLOW LINE continued, a wiring party every night. Hutments near BUS J 19. d 8.7. & at WARNIMONT WOODS handed over to 3rd Division, Took over NISSEN HUTMENTS at THE DELL J.17.c and at COUIN J 1. d. Section 2 moved from hutments near BUS J.19. d. 8.7. back to headquarters J 3. a. 7. 3.	P.C
	23.11.16		Work on YELLOW LINE continued. Two M. G. emplacements started. New arrangements re wiring YELLOW LINE. Section 2 in hutments at THE DELL & COUIN.	P.C
	24.11.16		All work stopped for wiring YELLOW LINE. Nos 1, 3, 4 section out wiring. M. G. dugouts continued	P.C
	25.11.16		Wiring continued.	
	26.11.16		Ditto Captain F. S. Collin returned to company from G.S. 31st division.	P.C
	27.11.16		"	
	28.11.16		"	
	29.11.16		"	P.C
	30.11.16		Wiring of YELLOW LINE completed	

P Cochran
Lt RE
for O.C 223rd Field Co

1875 Wt. W593/826 1,000,000 4/15 J.B.C. & A. A.D.S.S./Forms/C. 2118.

ORIGINAL.

CONFIDENTIAL.

WAR DIARY

of

223rd FIELD COMPANY.R.E

from 1/12/16 to 31/12/16.

VOLUME ~~XII.~~

Instructions regarding War Diaries and Intelligence Summaries are contained in F. S. Regs., Part II. and the Staff Manual respectively. Title Pages will be prepared in manuscript.

WAR DIARY

~~or~~

~~INTELLIGENCE SUMMARY~~

(Erase heading not required.)

Army Form C. 2118

223rd Field Co

Vol XII

Place	Date	Hour	Summary of Events and Information	Remarks and references to Appendices
COIGNEUX HUTS	1.12.16		A day off from the trenches. Men had baths. Section 2 moved to THE DELL and relieved Section 1, who returned to H.Q. at COIGNEUX. 2nd Lt COULTAS left on today's leave for ENGLAND. CAPT. F.S. COLLINS went to COUIN to act as C.R.E. Work on M.G. dug-out continued.	
J3.a.7.3			Work has been carried on as follows. Clearing YELLOW LINE between NAIRNES & GOTORIX. Clearing trenches E of HEBUTERNE KEEP. Clearing WOOD ST. through HEBUTERNE. Repairing billets in SAILLY and erecting necessary buildings and huts etc. in COUIN, 31d.	
	9.12.16			
	10.12.16		Work on M.G. dug-out continued & YELLOW LINE. Remainder of company had a holiday.	
	11.12.16		Work on THE KEEP HEBUTERNE resumed and also WOOD ST. also YELLOW LINE. Section 3 divided up to supervise the bunking of billets of the following villages FAMECHON, AUTHIE, St LEGER, COUIN. A shortage of material so not much progress made. Captain F.S. COLLINS returned from H.Q. on return of C.R.E. Repair of billets at SAILLY continued also Bde H.Q. dug-outs. Work at NISSEN Huts COUIN continued. M.G. Dug-out No 11 continued.	
	12.12.16		Work on THE KEEP and YELLOW LINE stopped and the two sections 2 & 4 taken off to wire R. LINE. The other work as on 11.12.16. Lt Lowe called in to advise R.F.A. on dug-out scheme.	
	13.12.16		Work as on 12.12.16 except M.G. No 10 dug-out was commenced. R.F.A. came to those for instruction. Captain F.S. COLLIN went on leave to ENGLAND.	
	14.12.16		Ditto.	
	15.12.16		" 2nd Lt H.W. COULTAS returned from leave.	
	16.12.16		Ditto.	
	17.12.16		Wiring of R. LINE completed. Lt COULTAS with 12 men went to live at THE KEEP HEBUTERNE. Work on YELLOW LINE commenced and also wiring ~~were~~ were THE KEEP HEBUTERNE. All other work as on 11.12.16. No 4 section returned to H.Q. from THE DELL and relieved No 1.	
	18.12.16		Work same as day before.	
	19.12.16		Bunking repairing billets FAMECHON, AUTHIE, St LEGER, COUIN, SAILLY. Erection of NISSEN HUTS COUIN 31d. M.G. Dug-outs 10 & 11 continued. Wiring KEEP.	
	22.12.16		and revetting YELLOW LINE. Supervising R.F.A. dug-outs.	
	23.12.16		All working parties off from KEEP & YELLOW LINE to dig cable trench through HEBUTERNE. Section I assist with their trench. Remainder of work carried on as day before. Strutting of cellars KEEP continued.	
	24.12.16		Ditto	
	25.12.16		A holiday. All working parties cancelled. Men had concert in evening.	
	26.12.16		Work carried on as on 24.12.16. Captain F.S. COLLIN returned from leave.	
	27.12.16		Ditto Captain F.S. COLLIN left company to take over command of 5th Field Squadron. He handed over to Capt P. Cochran	
	28.12.16		Work as on 24.12.16	
	29.12.16		Lieut W. INGHAM joined the company and took charge of Section 3. Work as before.	
	31.12.16		Work as on 24.12.16	P. Cochran Capt R.E. O.C. 223rd Field Co

1875 Wt. W593/826 1,000,000 4/15 J.B.C. & A. A.D.S.S./Forms/C. 2118.

HEADQUARTERS,
31ST
DIVISIONAL ENGINEERS.
No.
Date 5.2.17

Vol XI

Confidential

War Diary

of

223rd Field Company R.E.

from 1-1-17 to 31-1-17

Volume ~~13~~

Instructions regarding War Diaries and Intelligence Summaries are contained in F. S. Regs., Part II. and the Staff Manual respectively. Title Pages will be prepared in manuscript.

WAR DIARY
or
INTELLIGENCE SUMMARY
(Erase heading not required.)

223rd FIELD COY. R.E.

VOL. 13.

Army Form C. 2118

Place	Date	Hour	Summary of Events and Information	Remarks and references to Appendices
COIGNEUX.	1-1-17		HOLIDAY BY ORDER OF CORPS COMMANDER. Nos. 2 + 3 Sections change over work + billets. Capt. COCHRAN R.E. goes to G.H.Q. school for O.C's company course. Temporarily hands over command to Lt. F.W. MOORE R.E. Lt. W. RANKIN arrives as supernumerary officer	F.W.M.
	2-1-17		No 1 Sec. working HEBUTERNE KEEP. No. 2. Bunking Billets at SAILLY. ST. LEGER. AUTHIE. FAMECHON. No 3 Sec. on YELLOW LINE No. 4 Sec. COUIN HUTMENTS	F.W.M.
	3-1-17 4-1-17		No. 2 Sec. move to AMPLIER to work there + at SARTON + AUTHIEULE on BILLETS. OTHER SECTIONS work as above.	F.W.M.
	5-1-17 to 7-1-17		work as above.	F.W.M.
	8-1-17		Work on YELLOW LINE and COUIN stopped for this day + 3 + 4 Sections with 100 infantry have to immediately do 610 yds wire entanglement round CAT MILL.	F.W.M.
	9-10-1-17		Work as for 7-1-17 excepting no infantry parties available for work on YELLOW LINE and HEBUTERNE KEEP. CAPT. P. COCHRAN Returns + resumes command of Coy. on the 10th inst.	F.W.M.
	11.1.17.		Sec 1. Returned to H.Q. being relieved by section 4. 2Lt Bennett staff officer KEEP. HEBUTERNE. 31st Division relieved by 19th Division and this company become attached to 19th Division. Work carried on in YELLOW LINE with sappers only.	
	12.1.17.		Work on KEEP resumed. YELLOW LINE handed over to 51st F.C. Work on COUIN hutments resumed.	P.C
	13.1.17.		Work as on 12.1.17. Section 2 returned from AMPLIER men left at AUTHIE & FAMECHON to carry on bunking etc. remainder of section at H.Q.	
	14-1-17		work as on 13-1-17 also work commenced on HUTMENT CAMP at COIGNEUX Repairing Huts + bunking necessary buildings	F.W.M.
	15-1-17		work as on 14-1-17 also commenced on four Refilling points.	F.W.M.
	16-1-17 to 19-1-17		work as for 15-1-17.	F.W.M.
	20-1-17.		work as for 19-1-17. Capt. Cochran leaves the coy. temporarily on leave to England handing over to Capt. F.W. Moore RE	F.W.M.
	21-1-17 to 24-1-17		work as for 20-1-17.	F.W.M.
	25-1-17.		work as for 24-1-17 excepting R.P's Nos 1 + 2 finished + men from these recommence bunking at AUTHIE + ST LEGER	F.W.M.
	26-1-17 27-1-17		work as for 25-1-17	F.W.M.
	28-1-17		work as for 27-1-17 but R.P. no: 3 being completed men commence work on completion of NISSEN HUTMENT on BUS-ST LEGER Road	F.W.M.
	29-1-17 to 31-1-17		work as for 28-1-17.	F.W.M.

P. Cochran
Major R.E.
O.C. 223rd Field Co R.E.

1875 Wt. W593/826 1,000,000 4/15 J.B.C. & A. A.D.S.S./Forms/C. 2118.

HEADQUARTERS,
81ST
DIVISIONAL ENGINEERS.
No.
Date 1.3.17.

Vol 12

Original

Confidential
War Diary
of
223rd Field Company, R.E.
from 1/2/17 to 28/2/17

Vol. XIV

Instructions regarding War Diaries and Intelligence Summaries are contained in F. S. Regs., Part II. and the Staff Manual respectively. Title Pages will be prepared in manuscript.

WAR DIARY
or
INTELLIGENCE SUMMARY
(Erase heading not required.)

223rd Field Coy. R.E.

Army Form C. 2118

Vol. 14 I

Place	Date	Hour	Summary of Events and Information	Remarks and references to Appendices
COIGNEUX	1-2-17 to 2-2-17		HQrs. Sec. and No. 1. at COIGNEUX. No. 2 Sec. at AUTHIE and ST LEGER. No. 3 at SAILLY and No. 4. at HEBUTERNE all working in these areas.	
	3-2-17		Nos. 2 + 3 Sections rejoin HQrs at COIGNEUX. Capt COCHRAN rejoins + takes over command from Capt. Moore. 2nd Lieut R.V.M. BUCHANAN went on leave to ENGLAND	
"	4.2.17.		No 4 section return from KEEP HEBUTERNE to rejoin company. Day spent in preparation for departure next day.	
"	5.2.17.		Mounted section left COIGNEUX at 8.15.a.m and arrived BERNAVILLE at 4.30.PM. 9.a.m. No 1 section moved to ORVILLE and No 4 sec to VAUCHELLES to carry on work there. No 2 section & H.Q left at 1 PM by motor buses to BERNAVILLE. No 3 section ½ left at 1.30 PM by motor-buses to BERTEAUCOURT.	
BERNAVILLE.	6.2.17.		Recovered horse lines. Frost still continues, so unable to carry out cleaning of wagons. Corporal Howell goes to FRANQUEVILLE to superintend erection of NISSEN. HUT.	
	7.2.17.		12 men Sec 2 moved to FIEFFES to carry out repairs of old bath & fitting up new one.	
	8.2.17.		Preparations for another move.	
BONNEVILLE.	9.2.17		Left BERNAVILLE at 10 a.m, arrived BONNEVILLE at 12 noon. Remainder of No 2 section join H.Q from FIEFFES. Frost still continues. Lt W. RANKIN. left to be attached to C.E. Vth army.	P.C.
"	10.2.17.		No 1 section joined H.Q from ORVILLE. Had practice football match in afternoon.	P.C
"	11.2.17.		MEN had a holiday. In the afternoon football team went to BERNAVILLE and played 210th F. Co. We were beaten by 4 goals to 2. A very good game.	
"	12.2.17. 13.2.17		7 men of Section I went to BERNEUIL to assist TOWN.MAJOR. Frost still continues. 4 men proceeded for work at VALHEUREUX. SIDING	P.C
"	14.2.17.		2 men of Section I went to BERNEUIL to supervise work of German prisoners at BOISBIGOT. Played football match against Signals on our ground and we won after a good game by 4 goals to 2.	P.C
	15.2.17		Divisional Horse show at BERNAVILLE. We had four entries, but unsuccessful in gaining a prize. All turn-outs were very fine.	
	16.2.17.		Work carried on as usual. Played football match against EAST. LANCS in afternoon but were beaten by 6 goals to one. Lt COULTAS cut his knee & had to leave field. Ground very bad owing to thaw. 2nd Lt Buchanan returned from leave. 2nd Lt H.F. BARKER reported for duty.	P.C
	17.2.17.		Divisional R.E. sports at BERNAVILLE. Company did well 4 firsts and we second. Received warning notice for a move. Lt H.W. COULTAS went to hospital.	
	18.2.17		Section 3 returned to H.Q at BONNEVILLE, also detachments from BERNEUIL and VALHEUREUX. SIDING. All men on painting and packing wagons	P.C
"	19.2.17.		Preparations for a move still carried on, and all complete by night-fall,	
BEAUQUESNE.	20.2.17		Wet day. Parade at 10.30 Passed starting point opp BONNEVILLE CHURCH at 10.55. Roads very bad and heavy. Arrived BEAUQUESNE at 1.40 PM. where we went into billets. No horse-standings, but quite good billets.	P.C

1875 Wt. W593/826 1,000,000 4/15 J.B.C. & A. A.D.S.S./Forms/C. 2118.

Instructions regarding War Diaries and Intelligence Summaries are contained in F. S. Regs., Part II. and the Staff Manual respectively. Title Pages will be prepared in manuscript.

WAR DIARY or INTELLIGENCE SUMMARY

(Erase heading not required.)

223rd Field Co R E

VOL 14. II

Army Form C. 2118

Place	Date	Hour	Summary of Events and Information	Remarks and references to Appendices
J3 C 59	21.2.17		Parade at 8.45. Passed starting point just E of BEAUQUESNE at 9.5 a.m. Marched through MARIEUX. AUTHIE. ST. LEGER. COIGNEUX to old billets at J3 C 59. Roads very bad and heavy & No break-down in transport. Found 210th Field Co in occupation of billets. Very crowded and men had a very uncomfortable night. Also motor lorry with men's blankets stuck just outside MARIEUX, owing to bad condition of road.	PC
	22.2.17		Took over work formerly done by 82nd Field Co. R.E. Men employed in camp improving huts & commencing move. Motor lorry arrived at 12.30 PM	PC
"	23.2.17		Visited 93rd Bde and talked over scheme for work etc. Men still employed round camp. 4 men sent to HEBUTERNE as advance guard to take over billets in KEEP	PC
	24.2.17		Section 2 (20 men) moved into ~~billets~~ the KEEP. HEBUTERNE. Section 3 12 men commenced work in caves to make them habitable. 2nd Lt. Ingham working with left battalion 2nd Lt Buchanan with right battalion. Buchanan Staff Officer HEBUTERNE KEEP	PC
	25.2.17		News came that the GERMANS were retiring along the whole front of the V. corps. Our division occupied first three lines	PC
	26.2.17		2nd Lt Ingham and 2nd Lt Buchanan made a reconnaissance & report on two roads leading from HEBUTERNE at dawn. At 2 pm Sections 1 & 3 marched up to HEBUTERNE to live in caves. Section I went straight to work on Tramway running from K 10. c 55 to K 22 b 6 0. Section II went out to work on SUNKEN Rd and opened it as far as 16 POPLARS for pack transport by 10 P.M.	P.C
	27.2.17		Section 2 & 3 worked on road all day. Section I on Tramway. Section IV still at VAUCHELLES.	
	28.2.17		Work ditto. GOMMECOURT village occupied. Our lines still further advanced.	

P. Cochran
Major
O.C. 223rd (Field) Coy. R.E.

1875 Wt. W593/826 1,000,000 4/15 J.B.C. & A. A.D.S.S./Forms/C. 2118.

Confidential

HEADQUARTERS,
81ST
DIVISIONAL ENGINEERS.
No.
Date.

Vol 13

War Diary of Major P. Cochran R.E.
223rd Field Co R.E.

from 1st March 1917
to 31st March 1917 inclusive

Volume 15

Instructions regarding War Diaries and Intelligence Summaries are contained in F. S. Regs., Part II. and the Staff Manual respectively. Title Pages will be prepared in manuscript.

WAR DIARY
or
~~INTELLIGENCE SUMMARY~~
(Erase heading not required.)

223rd Field Co RE

Vol 15

Army Form C. 2118

Place	Date	Hour	Summary of Events and Information	Remarks and references to Appendices
83 C. 5. 9	1. 3. 17.		Section I still working on tramways living up in Caves HEBUTERNE. Sections 2 & 3. on SUNKEN RD. Section 4. VAUCHELLES. Germans still retiring. Capture of PUISIEUX.	
	2. 3. 17.		Ditto.	
	3. 3. 17.		Section I returned to H. Q at COIGNEUX. Section 2 & 3 still continued work on road.	
	4. 3. 17.		Section I had day in camp. Section 2 & 3 & 4. ditto	
Huts.	5. 3. 17.		Section I training, drill & strong points. Section 2 & 3 complete bridge over 1st German line. Artillery also working on road. 2nd Lt COULTAS returned from hospital. Lt RANKIN taken off strength transferred to Vth army. 2nd Lt BARKER supernumerary.	
COIGNEUX.	6. 3. 17.		Section I working up in HEBUTERNE improving billets. Section 2 & 3 continue with road. Section 4 returned to H. Q from VAUCHELLES.	
	7. 3. 17.		Section IV making billets in HEBUTERNE. Work as on 6th	
	8. 3. 17.		Ditto.	
	9. 3. 17.		Advanced party of Section IV 12 men went to live in HEBUTERNE. Work as usual.	
	10. 3. 17.		Section IV moved up to live in HEBUTERNE. to work on SUNKEN ROAD.	
	11. 3. 17.		HEBUTERNE handed over to 46th Division so sections 3. 3. 4 had to move out. The sections moved into German dug-outs in second line. Lt Bennett returned to H. Q sick. Dug-outs quite good but rather dirty. Work on road continued. Section I on repairs of billets COIGNEUX.	
	12. 3. 17.		Lt BARKER went up to take charge of Section IV. Work ditto.	
	13. 3. 17.		Work ditto.	
	14. 3. 17.		Received orders to be ready to concentrate at BOUQUEMAISON by 20th Division to be transferred to 1st Army.	
	15. 3. 17.		Section II returned to H. Q & handed over to Section III. Work on road continued. The following wire received at 5. PM. SP. 394. 15.3.17. Following wire received from SHIP. G954. aaa. Begins Possible that a move EAST may be ordered aaa The division is to be ready to move at 4 hours notice and men should be rested meanwhile aaa Orders as to working parties will be issued later aaa. Arrangements will be made to store surplus kit but all mobile ammunition tools and grenades will move [illegible] aaa 11 PM message received. Working parties as usual. All pontoon waggons & all men prepared for instant move	
	16. 3. 17.		Work on road continued. Men in camp Nos I & II sections resting and cleaning waggons.	
	17. 3. 17.		Movements orders received to transfer to 1st army. Attached to 92nd Bde for the move. No 3 & 4 sections returned to HQ arrived at 7. PM.	
	18. 3. 17.		All day spent on cleaning vehicles and harness. No 3 & IV sections had a bath.	
BEAUQUESNE.	19. 3. 17.		Left COIGNEUX at 9. 15 a m. arrived BEAUQUESNE at 2. 30 PM. Very slow and much interrupted march owing to coming across the line of march of 94th Bde. Billets. Fine day but very wet evening.	
BEAUVOIR	20. 3. 17.		Left. BEAUQUESNE at 8. a. m. Arrived ~~BEAUVOIR~~ 3. PM. Via DOULLENS. Again interrupted by 94th Bde. Billets. Fine but roads bad.	

1875 Wt. W593/826 1,000,000 4/15 J.B.C. & A. A.D.S.S./Forms/C. 2118.

Instructions regarding War Diaries and Intelligence Summaries are contained in F. S. Regs., Part II. and the Staff Manual respectively. Title Pages will be prepared in manuscript.

WAR DIARY
or
~~INTELLIGENCE SUMMARY~~

(Erase heading not required.)

223rd Field Co R.E.
Vol 15

Army Form C. 2118

Place	Date	Hour	Summary of Events and Information	Remarks and references to Appendices
BLANGERMONT.	21st March 1917		Left BEAUVOIR at 7.30. a.m. and arrived BLANGERMONT at 1 P.M. In billets. Very cold with some snow.	
FAUX.	22nd "		Left BLANGERMONT at 7.30 a.m. and reached FAUX VIA ST. POL. at 1.30. P.M. Very comfortable billets on main road. Weather still cold but dry. Roads in very good condition.	
"	23rd "		Day spent in cleaning wagons and equipment.	
FLECHINELLE.	24th		Left FAUX at 8.30. a.m. reached FLECHINELLE at 1 P.M. In billets again & very comfortable. Weather cold but dry. Summer time commenced 11 P.M. became 12 midnight	
ST. VENANT.	25th		Left FLECHINELLE at 8.45 a.m. reached ST. VENANT at 1.30. In billets along road. Quite comfortable.	
BERGUETTE Rd Billets	26th		Parade at 9. a.m. All huts inspected. Owing to question of our billets, stood too waiting to move. However billet question settled & we remained. Horse lines removed across road. Inoculation of the company commenced $\frac{TAB}{2}$. Section 1. inoculated.	
"	27th		Section 3 pontooning. Sect 4. Musketry & squad drill. Section 2 Trestle-bridging. Section 2 inoculated.	
"	28th		Section 3 " " 4. Works. repair horse lines La HAYE. " 3 & 4 inoculated.	
"	29th		Section 1 Works ditto. ~~Section 2~~ ~~pontooning~~.	
"	30th		Section 1 " " Section 2 pontooning.	
"	31st		Section 1 " " Drill musketry, strong points Section 3. Drill, musketry, strong points Section 4. Pontooning.	

P Cochran
Major R.E.
O.C. 223rd Field Co R.E.

1875 Wt. W593/826 1,000,000 4/15 J.B.C. & A. A.D.S.S./Forms/C. 2118.

Vol 14

CONFIDENTIAL

WAR DIARY.

OF

223rd FIELD COY R.E

APL 1st TO APL 30th 1917.

VOL XVI

Instructions regarding War Diaries and Intelligence Summaries are contained in F. S. Regs., Part II. and the Staff Manual respectively. Title Pages will be prepared in manuscript.

WAR DIARY
or
INTELLIGENCE SUMMARY
(Erase heading not required.)

Army Form C. 2118

223rd Field Co R.E.
Vol 16.

Place	Date	Hour	Summary of Events and Information	Remarks and references to Appendices
ST VENANT. Billets	1st April '17		Had usual inspections. Church parade for coy at 11.15 a.m.	
BERGUETTE R.d	2nd		Training continued. Section I pontooning. C.R.E's conference. Received warning order for move to area of CANADIAN CORPS.	
"			Received orders to move to GOUY.SERVINS halting one night at BETHUNE. Left ST VENANT at 2.30 PM. reached BETHUNE at 6 PM	
BETHUNE. Billets.	3rd			
GOUY.SERVINS. TENTS and HUTS. RE yard.	4th		Left BETHUNE at 9 a.m. reached GOUY.SERVINS at 2. PM. men in billets for one night except drivers & H.Q. Tents pitched & camp formed W of yard.	
	4th 5th 6th 7th		} all coy on road leading from Windmill to R.E. yard Work delayed owing to lack of motor lorries.	
	8th		Lt BARKER & 6 sappers supervising work on main road through GOUY-SERVINS.	
	9th		Work on road continued. Capture of VIMY RIDGE	
Under Canvas near LAMOTTE. FARM	10th		Received orders from TOWN MAJOR GOUY to move to LA. MOTTE. FARM. MONT. ST. ELOY This order verified by C.E. CANADIAN CORPS Moved to LAMOTTE FARM in afternoon. Roads bad & crowded with transport. Capt Moore & Lt BARKER left with transport at GUOY.	Under C.E. 1st Army for work on water supply.
MONT. ST ELOY	11th 12th		} awaited orders from 1st Army Water Supply officer. Capt MOORE went to hospital. rose measles. Very heavy fall of snow 4"	
	13th 14th		} Officers surveying pipe-lines & pumping stations and arranging for new schemes & work commenced at Reservoir La MOTTE	
	15th		Wet day. Section I moved to NEUVILLE, ST VAAST Section 2 & 3 to CARENCY. Mounted section from GUOY to LA. MOTTE. FARM. Received orders afterwards to move back to Division. Matter referred to XIII CORPS Destination altered to ECOIVRES.	
ECOIVRES HUTMENTS.	16th		Moved H.Q. to hutments at ECOIVRES. Section also returned to join H.Q. at ECOIVRES. Work under C.E. XIII Corps.	
" "	17th		Gen General work. Dismantling & transportation of NISSEN HUTS. Repairs to billets Work in shops etc	
	18th		Capt F.W. MOORE returned from hospital	
	19th 20th 21st		} Work ditto.	

1875 Wt. W593/826 1,000,000 4/15 J.B.C. & A. A.D.S.S./Forms/C. 2118.

Instructions regarding War Diaries and Intelligence Summaries are contained in F. S. Regs., Part II. and the Staff Manual respectively. Title Pages will be prepared in manuscript.

WAR DIARY
or
INTELLIGENCE SUMMARY
(Erase heading not required.)

223rd Field Co RE
Vol 16

Army Form C. 2118

Place	Date	Hour	Summary of Events and Information	Remarks and references to Appendices
Ecoivres.	22nd April		General work repairs to billets etc. Very good weather. All wagons repainted	Under C.E. XIII Corps
HUTMENTS	29th		Received orders to take over work of 247th Field Co RE (63rd Division) in line just N of ARRAS.	
Bivouacs at 9.9.b.3.3. N of ST NICHOLAS.	30th		Moved from ECOIVRES to 9.9.b.3.3. Roads very dusty. Sections 3 & 4 moved up to dug-outs & gunpits at H4.c. just SW of GAVRELLE.	

P Cochran
Major RE
O.C. 223rd Field Co RE

1875 Wt. W593/826 1,000,000 4/15 J.B.C. & A. A.D.S.S./Forms/C. 2118.

ORIGINAL

C O N F I D E N T I A L.

WAR DIARY

of

223rd FIELD COMPANY R.E.

from May 1st, 1917 to May 31st, 1917

Volume XVII

* * * * * * * * * *

Instructions regarding War Diaries and Intelligence Summaries are contained in F. S. Regs., Part II. and the Staff Manual respectively. Title Pages will be prepared in manuscript.

WAR DIARY or INTELLIGENCE SUMMARY

(Erase heading not required.)

223rd Field Co R.E.

Vol 17

Army Form C. 2118

Place	Date	Hour	Summary of Events and Information	Remarks and references to Appendices
H.Q Bivouacs at G.9.b 6.2.	1st May	1917.	Nos 3 & 4 Sections at H4.C. in gun-pits. Dug-outs cleared and R.E. stores salvaged & dump formed at POINT DU JOUR. Conference held at Div H.Q. in view of future offensive operations, this company attached to 93rd Bde H.Q.	
	2nd May		Line reconnoitred. Section 3 & 4 obtained their place in Assembly Trench. 2 platoons KOYLI attached to these sections for the construction of strong-points. Sections 1 & 2 moved at night to H1.d.3.2. to be in reserve. Sections 3 & 4 & KOYLI moved into assembly trenches at 11. P.M. 6C company went to Adv Bde H.Q at H.3.d.1.9. Y day.	
	3rd May		Z day. Zero 3.45. a.m. Enemy's barrage opened 30 secs afterwards. No news from right flank & 2Lt Ingham sent forward at 5.30 a.m. to see whether he could start his strong point. Not possible so returned to hold support line. Affairs appeared very critical at 7 a.m. as batt in support had been used up to reinforce. The Support line held by 2 sections RE. and 2 Platoons KOYLI. At 4.30. P.M. section recalled & managed to escape without casualties. One platoon KOYLI remained all night to reinforce 15th W. Yorks. At 7. P.M. Bde received orders to put their whole reserve Batt on working party & establish line as suggested. Orders for this work were issued at 8.30 P.M. Sections 1 & 2 were called up from Reserve for this work. Very little was done owing to the heavy shelling and the uncertainty of the position. Working parties suffered some casualties and Section 2 had Sergt Whitehead severely wounded.	
	4th May		Section 3 & 4 out at night reconnoitring for new support line. Bde relief took place & commenced work on S.C.T. with KOYLI.	
	5th May		Section 3 & 4 marked out Support line & supervised work on South C.T.	
	6th May		Sections 1.3 & 4 commenced Support line at C 25. c. 5.3. Completed four fire-bays as posts.	
	6th May		Section 2, returned to H.Q. Elephant shelters erected in RAILWAY cutting for one section.	
	7th May		Section 1 erecting shelters. Baths at St CATHERINE commenced by Section 2.	
	8th		Work continued on Support line & C.T's.	
	9th			
	10th		Section 2 relieved Section 3 on right sector. } Work carried on the same	
	11th		Section 1 relieved Section 4 – left sector }	
	12th		Captain Moore R.E. relieved 6 C at Cutting.	
	13th		Work as usual. Commencement of work on tramway from POINT DU JOUR to Support Line.	
	14th		Section 3 relieved Sec 4 at the CUTTING. Sec 4 returned to H.Q. to work on baths.	
	15th			
	16th		} Work in line carried on. Very heavy shelling hindered this work a great deal. 2nd Lt BARKER relieved 2nd Lt COULTAS.	
	17th			
	18th			
	19th		Division relieved. Co relieved by 247 F. Co. R.E. No 1 & 2 Sections returned to H.Q. from gun-pits. Sec 3 from Cutting.	

1875 Wt. W593/826 1,000,000 4/15 J.B.C. & A. A.D.S.S./Forms/C. 2118.

Army Form C. 2118

Instructions regarding War Diaries and Intelligence Summaries are contained in F. S. Regs., Part II. and the Staff Manual respectively. Title Pages will be prepared in manuscript.

WAR DIARY
or
INTELLIGENCE SUMMARY 223rd Field Co. RE.
(Erase heading not required.)

VOL 17.

Place	Date	Hour	Summary of Events and Information	Remarks and references to Appendices
ECOIVRES. HUTMENTS.	20th May.		Moved back to the same hutments as we left on 30th APRIL. Took over work of 248th F. Co and employed under CORPS. Marched in afternoon. Transport went separate. Dismounted by cross-country track.	
	21st May.		The following work was commenced. Dismantling of X. Hutments. Repairs to Reinforcement Camp. Improvements & extension to Rifle Range F 20. C. Central. Repairing accomodation at Labour Group H. Q. General work in workshops. Constructing new shed at H. A. Hd Qrs. Erection of latrines in ECOIVRES.	
	22nd May		Captain F. W. Moore proceeded on leave for England.	
	22nd, 23rd, 24th, 25th, 26th, 27th		Work ditto.	
	28th		Dismantling of X. hutments completed.	
	30th		Commenced work on wells at BETHONSART.	
	31st		Work ditto	

P. Cochran
Major RE
O.C. 223rd Field Co RE

1875 Wt. W593/826 1,000,000 4/15 J.B.C. & A. A.D.S.S./Forms/C. 2118.

ORIGINAL.

CONFIDENTIAL.

WAR DIARY

of

223rd Field Company.R.E.

from 1st June.1917 to June 30th.1917.

VOLUME XVIII

Instructions regarding War Diaries and Intelligence Summaries are contained in F. S. Regs., Part II. and the Staff Manual respectively. Title Pages will be prepared in manuscript.

WAR DIARY
or
INTELLIGENCE SUMMARY
(Erase heading not required.)

223rd Field Co R.E.
Vol 18.

Army Form C. 2118

Place	Date	Hour	Summary of Events and Information	Remarks and references to Appendices
ECOIVRES. Hutments.	1. 6. 17.		Commenced work on increase of accomodation at BRAY. Work on rifle range continued. 6 men at BETHONSART on Wells and latrines. Various odd jobs for C.R.E.C.T.	
	5. 6. 17.		Captain F.W. Moore returned from leave. 2nd Lt S. G. Bennett went on leave to England. Work ditto.	
	7. 6. 17.		Amongst the list of recipients of Military Crosses given in Birthday honours, was the name of Captain F. W. Moore. Commenced preparations for horse-show.	
	8. 6. 17.		Company under orders to proceed back to line. All work possible completed and no new work commenced.	
G 9 d 3 7	9. 6. 17.		Relieved 247th Field Co in line in Rt Bde sector. GAVRELLE. Sections 3 & 4 marched straight to gun-pits and take over work. 6 C with 2nd Lt BUCHANAN at the Cutting with 12 men from sections 3 & 4. H Q 1 & 2 sections established a camp at G 9. d. 3 7.	
	10 6. 17.		Line reconnoited in early morning. Very quiet and not a shot fired. No 3 section commenced work on right sub-sector and No 4 on the left. Work purely maintenace and widening trenches. Brigade weak in consequence only small working parties available. Commenced dug-out in Support Line.	
	16 6. 17.		Sections relieved. Sections 1 & 2 to gun-pits. Sec 3 to cutting & Sec 4 to H. Q. 2nd Lt S. G. BENNETT received orders to proceed to War Office to report for service to India. In consequence struck off strength. 2nd Lt W. INGHAM went on leave to England. Work on line continued, also dug-out for Gunners at B.P.C. 317 continued. Erecting shelter for G. O. C 93rd Bde in Cutting.	
	17. 6. 17.		Corporal W. Pickard severely wounded by a shell on GAVRELLE. RD (Died of wounds 18th)	
	18. 6. 17.		Divisional Horse Show. Tool-cart 1st Prize. Pontoon 3rd Prize. Section jumping, 1st Prize. Waggons looked very well.	
	20. 6. 17		Corps Horse Show. Tool-cart & Pontoon Waggon 3rd [illegible] in each event. Received special consolation prize from C.E. XIII Corps for mules in Tool cart. Received special prize from C. R. E. for Pontoon. 5th Division won. Section jumpers did not do well. Missed the course first time round. 21st 2nd Lt P. G. JONES joins for duty.	
	22. 6. 17.		Sections relieved. Section 1. remains at gun pits. Section 2 returns to H. Q. Sec 3 to Cutting. Sec 4 to gun-pits	

1875 Wt. W593/826 1,000,000 4/15 J.B.C. & A. A.D.S.S./Forms/C. 2118.

Instructions regarding War Diaries and Intelligence Summaries are contained in F. S. Regs., Part II. and the Staff Manual respectively. Title Pages will be prepared in manuscript.

WAR DIARY
or
INTELLIGENCE SUMMARY
(Erase heading not required.)

Army Form C. 2118

223rd Field Co R.E.

Vol 18.

Place	Date	Hour	Summary of Events and Information	Remarks and references to Appendices
C9d 3.7.			Work much the same, except work concentrated on Bde left sub-sector FOX VALLEY and MARINE.	
	22nd 6.17		Captain F. W. MOORE relieved O.C. & took over forward work.	
	26.6.17		Sapper BENSLEY slightly wounded. Dug 3 dummy assembly trenches S of TOWY.	
	27th 6.17		Sections relieved. Section 1 to H.Q. Sect 2 to gun pits. Sec 3 to gun pits. Sec 4 to Cutting. 2nd Lt W. Ingham returned from leave.	
	28.6.17 – 30.6.17		Work in line continued. Rear work improvements to baths at ST CATHERINES and completion of officers' bath.	
			2Lt H. W. COULTAS went on leave to ENGLAND.	

P Cochran
Major RE
O.C. 223rd Field Co R.E.

1875 Wt. W593/826 1,000,000 4/15 J.B.C. & A. A.D.S.S./Forms/C. 2118.

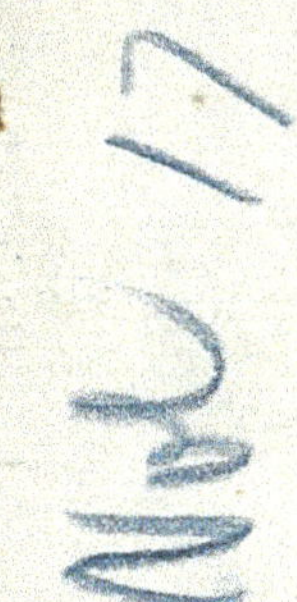

ORIGINAL.

CONFIDENTIAL.

WAR DIARY

of

223rd Field Company.R.E.

July 1st to July 31st.1917

VOLUME ~~XVIII~~ XIX

* * * * * * * * * * *

Instructions regarding War Diaries and Intelligence Summaries are contained in F. S. Regs., Part II. and the Staff Manual respectively. Title Pages will be prepared in manuscript.

WAR DIARY
or
INTELLIGENCE SUMMARY
(Erase heading not required.)

Army Form C. 2118

223rd Field Co R.E.
Vol 19.

Place	Date	Hour	Summary of Events and Information	Remarks and references to Appendices
G.9d 3.7.	July 1st	1917.	No1 Section H.Q. Nos 2 & 3 Sections Gun-pits. No4. Section at CUTTING. Work in line hindered through heavy shelling.	
			Work continued on baths ST CATHERINE'S	
	" 3rd	—	Preparations made for change of camp to take over 211th CAMP. Forward work taken over by 247th Field Co. All sections returned to H.Q. for one night. Baths at ST CATHERINE'S completed with new settling tank and exit.	
G.10b. 8.2.	" 4th		Took over camp of 211th Field Co & dump. Company moved over in morning. Took over work on RED. LINE.	
	" 6th		Commenced work on RED. LINE. 1 Battalion 15th W.Y.R. & 2 coys 18 W.Y.R. as working parties. No1 section working on left between OUSE. SIDING and OUSE. ALLEY. No4 section working on excavation for shelters and new fire trench S of BAILLEUL. EAST. POST.	
	" 7th			
	" 8th		Work ditto. Good work done by infantry.	
	" 9th		Had nights rest.	
	" 10th		Work resumed. Erection of shelters commenced. 2nd Lt Buchanan went to BOULOGNE on four days leave.	
	" 11th		Work stopped owing to warning order for a move. Had company sports. Very successful & good sportsmanship showed	
	" 12th		Lt COULTAS returned from leave. Had company concert. All waggons packed preparatory to a move.	
	" 13th		Relieved the 2nd CANADIAN. ENGINEERS. at A8c.3.8. In reserve. Move completed by 3. P.M. Work commenced on improvement of Div H.Q. at F6c Central. Took over a very good camp with good accomodation. 2nd Lt R.V.M. BUCHANAN. returned from BOULOGNE.	
	14th		Work commenced on Div. Hdqrs. + one section sent to R.E. Dump to work for C.R.E. (No 2 Sec).	[initials]
	15th–16th		Work as for 14th. Major P. Cochran R.E. goes on leave to England on 16th handing over command temporarily to Capt F.W. [illegible] RE.	[initials]
	17th 19th		Work as above, but work on Div. Cinema commenced at NEUVILLE ST VAAST.	[initials]
	20th–21st		Work as above but party of 30 men work on building huts at MT. ST ELOY for these two days only being then taken off. Section 4 relieves Sec. 2 at R.E Dump on 21st. Sec. Lieut. H.F BARKER proceeds on leave to England on 21st. Coy. Under [illegible] Standing Orders	[initials]
	22nd		Work at Div. Hdqrs almost complete + the men released work on Rifle Range at MONT ST ELOY + Div. Gas School	[initials]
	23rd 25th		Work as above. Sec. 4. rejoin Company from RE Dump on 25th.	[initials]
	26th 27th		Work as above.	[initials]
	28th–30th		Work as above, but work also commenced at site of New Divisional Hdqrs. on 28th.	[initials]
	31st		Work all as above for 30th. Major P. Cochran R.E. returns from leave, resumes Command of Company	[initials]

P. Cochran
Major R.E.
O.C. 223rd Field Co R.E.

1875 Wt. W593/826 1,000,000 4/15 J.B.C. & A. A.D.S.S./Forms/C. 2118.

ORIGINAL.

Vol 18

C O N F I D E N T I A L.

WAR DIARY

of

223rd Field Company.R.E.

from 1/8/17 to 31/8/17.

VOLUME XX.

* * * * * * * * * *

Army Form C. 2118

Instructions regarding War Diaries and Intelligence Summaries are contained in F. S. Regs., Part II. and the Staff Manual respectively. Title Pages will be prepared in manuscript.

WAR DIARY
or
INTELLIGENCE SUMMARY
(Erase heading not required.)

223rd Field Co R. E.
Vol 20

Place	Date	Hour	Summary of Events and Information	Remarks and references to Appendices
	1.8.17.		Work continued on Div H.Q. Cinema. ST. ELOI. baths. Winter horse-lines. New C.T. over Ridge to Petit VIMY.	
AUX. RIETZ	2.8.17.		Very heavy rain. Work delayed. 2nd Lt. H.T. BARKER returned from leave.	
G.10.b.8.2.	3.8.17.		Work ditto. On new C.T. over VIMY. RIDGE. Corps cavalry and D. COY A.&S.H (5th Div) employed.	
	5.8.17.		2nd Lieut. R.V.M. BUCHANAN went on leave to ENGLAND. Lt. COULTAS took charge of horse-standings	
	8.8.17.		Supervised bunking ~~in~~ billets at MT. ST ELOY. Work on D.H.Q. continued, also CINEMA.	
	10.8.17		Two sappers attached R.F.A. to fix gas blankets. Making ovens for 93rd Field Ambulance. CINEMA completed. Constructing trench mortar emplacements.	
	16.8.17.		½ Coy employed on D.H.Q. Building new hut for G.O.C. and Signals. Erecting NISSEN. HUT.S. and lining old huts with canvas. Partitions inserted where required. Work delayed by weather and alterations. 2nd Lt. P. G JONES interviewed for purpose of obtaining a transfer to Flying Corps as observer.	
			Commenced to ~~h~~ erect stage at Divisional CINEMA.	
	17.8.17		2nd Lt. R.V.M. BUCHANAN returned from leave.	
	17.8.17		Work on C.T. over VIMY completed, except for few extra screens, latrines and steps.	
	18.8.17		Corps Cavalry and A&S.H under the supervision of 2nd Lt. BARKER commenced work on RED.LINE. at T.20. b.5.4. (about.) An old trench did exist, but this required widening and draining and shelters erected.	
	21.8.17		Stage and dressing rooms completed at CINEMA.	
	22.8.17.		Work at D.H.Q continued and completed on 28.8.17.	
	28.8.17		Very heavy storm of wind and rain. Various repairs had to be carried out next day.	
	29.8.17.		Work on REDLINE continued. Erecting NISSEN HUTS at E Yorks horse-standings.	
	30.8.17		Repairs to bicycles & tools carried out in camp in preparation for a move.	

P Cochran Major R.E.
O.C. 223rd (Field) Coy. R.E.

1875 Wt. W593/826 1,000,000 4/15 J.B.C. & A. A.D.S.S./Forms/C. 2118.

ORIGINAL

Vol 19

CONFIDENTIAL.

WAR DIARY

of

223rd Field Company. R.E.

from 1/9/17 to 30/9/17.

VOLUME XXI

==*=*=*=*=*=*=*=*=

Army Form C. 2118

Instructions regarding War Diaries and Intelligence Summaries are contained in F. S. Regs., Part II. and the Staff Manual respectively. Title Pages will be prepared in manuscript.

WAR DIARY
or
INTELLIGENCE SUMMARY
(Erase heading not required.)

223rd Field Co R.E.

Vol 21.

Place	Date	Hour	Summary of Events and Information	Remarks and references to Appendices
AUX. RIETZ G.10.b.8.2.	1.9.17.		Work on RED LINE continued until the 4th when the A&S.H. returned to join their division. Good work done on this portion about 470 yds completed. Commenced work on a new Div H.Q. just south of ECURIE RAILHEAD on the Polo ground. On 3rd commenced work on our new transport lines near ECURIE, preparing accomodation. Erecting NISSEN HUTS for drivers and 1 section.	
A18 b 8.6	6.9.17		Moved camp. Handed over to 7th Field Co 3rd Canadian Division and took over work and billets of 491 Field Co. RE. 5th Division. Marched over whole company to ECURIE, and completed NISSEN HUTS sufficient for two officers ~~and~~ 1 section and the Drivers. In afternoon Sections 1.2 & 4 marched up to RIDGE and took over accomodation in trenches occupied by 491. Section 3 remained at camp to continue work on D.H.Q.	
	7.9.17.		Reconnoitred line and arranged work. 93rd Bde relieved 95th Bde in the line during afternoon.	
	8.9.17.		Work commenced on draining TIRED ALLEY and raising trench boards there. No infantry available. Work commenced on wiring in front of BRITANNIA TRENCH. 164 infantry employed. Good work was done on this wiring for five nights. Section 2 moved up to Orchard Dug-out.	
	9.9.17.		Work on TIRED continued and work commenced on ARLEUX LOOP, draining and widening. Relaying trench boards. Commenced work on A.D.S. near TUNNEL DUMP just W of BAILLEUL. Men also employed in improvement of Brigade H.Q. Section 4 employed on work W of RED LINE. Section 1 working on TIRED & on ARLEUX LOOP. Work continued just the same except infantry left to do their own wiring. 2nd Lt Jones acted as adviser in the direction of the wire. Work was done on improvement of the Wells in ARLEUX, and the closing of one declared unfit for use.	
	✱		Section 3 still employed on D.H.Q. also erecting huts in transport lines.	
	11.9.17.		Work on D.H.Q. stopped site condemned. D.H.Q. to be in the same place as the former division had. 10 men employed in improving accomodation there. Work done on horse-standings covering same with C.I.	

1875 Wt. W593/826 1,000,000 4/15 J.B.C. & A. A.D.S.S./Forms/C. 2118.

Instructions regarding War Diaries and Intelligence Summaries are contained in F. S. Regs., Part II. and the Staff Manual respectively. Title Pages will be prepared in manuscript.

WAR DIARY
or
INTELLIGENCE SUMMARY
(Erase heading not required.)

Army Form C. 2118

223rd Field Co. R E

Vol 21

Place	Date	Hour	Summary of Events and Information	Remarks and references to Appendices
A 18. 6 8. 6	12.9.17		Work continued. Section 3 employed on improving existing D. H. Q as taken over ~~by~~ from 0th Division. Erection of NISSEN HUTS for camp continued. Also work on horse-standings.	
	"		Section 1, still working on TIRED. ALLEY. Section 2 on ARLEUX. LOOP. Excavation of BARON. TRENCH. commenced.	
	"		Section 4 on intermediate work. A. D. S. erection of clothes store and changing room. Commenced canteen at Daylight Railhead	
	17.9.17.		Reconnaissance made of dug-outs and wells in Rt Bde area.	
ECURIE.	18.9.17.		Capt Moore M. C. went on leave to ENGLAND. 19-9.17 – 29.9.17. 6C. returned to Transport line, and made H. Q there	
A 27 6. 8. 3	19.9.17.		Sections relieved. Sec 1. to transport lines. Sec 2 to intermediate camp at B.19.a 7 5 Sec 3 to intermediate camp. Sec 4 to Orchard Dug-out. 93rd Inf Bde relieved 92nd Inf Bde in Rt. Bde area.	
	20.9.17.		The following work commenced and continued. Supervision of NISSEN. HUTS for 93rd Inf Bde. Dummy tank, horse, standings. Erecting NISSEN. HUTS at D. H. Q for H A G. A. D. S. Brigade. H. Q new ~~$~~ shelter. Canteen. Daylight Railhead. Work on the following trenches. TIRED. ALLEY. BARUN and ARLEUX. LOOP. Fixing up new windlasses for wells in ARLEU X, and gas blankets ~~and~~ frames in dug-outs.	
	24.9.17		Work on TIRED. ALLEY complete. Erecting NISSEN. HUTS for 93rd Bde complete. Section 4 cook-house knocked out by shell fire, no one hurt. Sec 4 moved to dug-out in RED LINE. Section 3 moved up to this dug-out on 25th	
	26.9.17.		Daylight Railhead canteen complete, also work on D. H. Q and Brigade H. Q.	
	27.9.17.		Work commenced on PRINCE'S. STREET. Trench, necessary to use V frames. Work commenced on new cinema. 1 N CO. 9 11 OR proceed to AC Q to pull down French Hut for this purpose.	
	28.9.17		Commenced work on soup kitchen at B.15.C.5.2.	
	30.9.17.		Dummy tank completed. Sec4 returned to transport lines to take over work of Section 1.	

P. Cochran
Major R.E.
O. C. 223rd Field Co R.E.

1875 Wt. W593/826 1,000,000 4/15 J.B.C. & A. A.D.S.S./Forms/C. 2118.

Vol 20

C O N F I D E N T I A L.
==*=*=*=*=*=*=*=*=*=*

W A R   D I A R Y

of

223rd Field Company. R.E.

October 1st.,1917 to October 31st.,1917.

VOLUME   XXII

Instructions regarding War Diaries and Intelligence Summaries are contained in F. S. Regs., Part II. and the Staff Manual respectively. Title Pages will be prepared in manuscript.

WAR DIARY ~~or~~ ~~INTELLIGENCE SUMMARY~~

(Erase heading not required.)

223rd Field Company R.E.

Army Form C. 2118

Vol 22

Place	Date	Hour	Summary of Events and Information	Remarks and references to Appendices
ECURIE A 27. b 8 3.		1. 10. 17.	Sections relieved. Sec's 1 & 2 to RED. LINE. dug-out for work in forward areas. Section I working on the right and Sec 2 on the left. Sec 3 moved from forward to intermediate billets B19. a. 7. 5. 92nd Inf Bde relieved 93rd Inf Bde in Rt Brigade sector.	
			The following work commenced and continued. Laying trench-boards and draining ARLEUX. LOOP and BARON. Trenches. Erecting U frames and revetting Prince's Trench. Completing entrances of A.D.S. TUNNEL DUMP. Soup Kitchen erection. Dismantling of French hut ACQ. Horse-standings. New CINEMA ECURIE. Fixing gas blankets to dug-outs	
		4. 10. 17	Captain F. W MOORE. M.C. RE. returned from leave. Took over supervision of work up the line on the 6th	
		6. 10 17	Soup kitchen completed. Work done on R. F. A. tracks	
		10. 10. 17.	Work on A.D.S completed. 2Lt P. G. JONES went on leave to ENGLAND. 10th–20th Corporal Griffiths and two sappers wounded by shell in PRINCES	
		11. 10. 17.	2Lt L. F. PAGET. reported for duty. Company now with an officers strength of 8.	
			Assisting 92nd & 93rd Bde with erection of NISSEN. HUTS. at TRANSPORT. LINES	
			Horse put under cover on 10th owing to the wild weather. Strong winds and heavy rains. Ground around camp very muddy.	
		12. 10. 17.	Section 2 moved from RED. LINE. to H. Q ECURIE.	
		13. 10. 17.	Sections relieved. Section 1 from RED LINE to intermediate billets. Section 3 from intermediate billets to RED LINE and took over work of Section 1. Section 4 from H. Q to RED. LINE. and took over work of Section 2.	
		14. 10. 17.	The following work commenced and continued. (1) The following trenches worked on. ARLEUX. LOOP. BARON. PRINCE'S. ST. SEVERN. Erection of shelters commenced in BARON. Kitchen for A.D.S. New CINEMA. ECURIE. ERECTION of NISSEN HUTS in transport lines. R.F.A. Tracks	
		15. 10. 17	50 infantry attached to assist in creation of ½ battalion camp at ECURIE. Work commenced on this day. SAP. VICKERS. killed and Sergt CHAPMAN wounded.	
		16. 10. 17	Commenced work on coal-bins urgently required at ROCLINCOURT. Lt COULTAS left for AIRE to attend course on heavy bridging.	
			Received word that 2Lt. P. G. JONES was accepted for flying corps.	
			Commenced work on investigation for entrance to subterranean passage between ARLEUX. and BOIS. BERNARD	
		20. 10. 17.	Coal bins completed. Kitchen for A.D.S. completed.	
			Sand-bagging around entrance of wells in ARLEUX. completed	
		22. 10. 17.	2nd Lt P. G. JONES returned from leave and left, on 23rd to join R. F. C	
		24. 10. 17.	Trench boarding and revetting of PRINCE'S completed as far as BARON	
			Section 3 moved down to H. Q at ECURIE.	

Instructions regarding War Diaries and Intelligence Summaries are contained in F. S. Regs., Part II. and the Staff Manual respectively. Title Pages will be prepared in manuscript.

WAR DIARY
or
~~INTELLIGENCE SUMMARY~~
(Erase heading not required.)

Army Form C. 2118

223rd Field Company R.E.
Vol 22.

Place	Date	Hour	Summary of Events and Information	Remarks and references to Appendices
ECURIE.	25.10.17.		Sections relieved. Sec 1. to RED.LINE.dug-out. Sec 2 from H.Q to REDLINE. Sec 4. from RED.LINE. to intermediate camp. Concrete road closed to RIDGE. Had difficulty to get waggons to intermediate camp.	
A27. b.8.3.	26.10.17		Intermediate camp abandoned and Section 4 moved back to H.Q. Work carried on as before.	
	27.10.17		Sergeant A. Chapman awarded the Military Medal for:- Consistent good work in front trenches, and conspicuous coolness and bravery under fire.	
			Made 2 dummy guns for R.F.A.	
			Commenced work on BRITANNIA.TRENCH. also gumboot store and shelters at Longwood, and dug-out at BATTALION H.Q TUNNEL. Erecting NISSEN. HUTS for R.F.A. and D.A.C.	
	30.10.17		Lt H.W COULTAS returned from Heavy Bridging School AIRE	

P. Cochran
Major R.E.
O.C. 223rd Field Co R.E.

1875 Wt. W593/826 1,000,000 4/15 J.B.C. & A. A.D.S.S./Forms/C. 2118.

ORIGINAL.

Vol 21

CONFIDENTIAL.

War Diary

of

223rd Field Company.R.E.

From 1/11/17 to 30/11/17.

Volume XXIII

==*=*=*=*=*=*

Instructions regarding War Diaries and Intelligence Summaries are contained in F. S. Regs., Part II. and the Staff Manual respectively. Title Pages will be prepared in manuscript.

WAR DIARY
or
INTELLIGENCE SUMMARY
(Erase heading not required.)

Army Form C. 2118

223rd Field Co. R.E.
Vol 23.

Place	Date	Hour	Summary of Events and Information	Remarks and references to Appendices
ECURIE. A 27 b. 8. 3.	1.11.17.		Work continued. 1 N.C.O. and 11 sappers went to BRAY to complete and improve Battalion camp. Work commenced on canteen ECURIE Railhead.	
	3.11.17		4 N.C.O's and 12 sappers joined 11th East Yorks to practice for taking part in a raid. Sappers to carry mobile charges for destruction of dug-outs. Charges carried one 20 lb and one 10 lb. 1 N.C.O. and 3 sappers attached to each of the four companies going over.	
	5.11.17.		Lt Buchanan in charge of dummy attack opposite Fresnoy Wood. Carried up stores and figures night of the 6th.	
	7.11.17.		At night Lt Buchanan fixed dummy figures in front of front line parapet distance x 5 - 10 yds out, and arranged two bangalore torpedoes.	
	8.11.17.		Raid took place just North of Fresnoy, on German 2nd line. The raid a great success, 21 prisoners captured. The sappers did very well and destroyed 14 German dug-outs, most of them with the enemy in. One concrete M G emplacement, one minenwerfer, one S.A.A dump two traverses. More charges taken over than there were places to destroy. Casualties were one missing and one slightly wounded. The men who took part in the raid were Corporal Hampshire, Sappers. Swales, Gough, Drake (No 1 Section); Corporal Stanley, sapper Calvert, Leayle, Brayshaw: Corporal Fletcher, Sappers, Sykes, Radcliffe, Earnshaw; Corporal Johnson, Sappers, Hemingway, Stevenson, Houldin. Corporal Hampshire was reported missing and is believed to have been killed. Congratulations on the success of the raid received from Army, Corps and Divisional commanders	
			Dummy attack on Fresnoy met with great success M G fire attracted 10 secs after figures were raised Figures lowered after one minute. One set of figures refused to drop and Lt Buchanan crawled out amidst heavy M. G. fire and pushed them down. All men working figures (Section 2) returned safely.	
	8.11.17.		Sections relieved. Sections 1 & 2 to H. Q. ECURIE and 3 & 4 to RED LINE.	
	10.11.17.		The men taking part in raid returned to H. Q. and employed on work in camp.	

1875 Wt. W593/826 1,000,000 4/15 J.B.C. & A. A.D.S.S./Forms/C. 2118.

Instructions regarding War Diaries and Intelligence Summaries are contained in F. S. Regs., Part II. and the Staff Manual respectively. Title Pages will be prepared in manuscript.

WAR DIARY or INTELLIGENCE SUMMARY

(Erase heading not required.)

Army Form C. 2118

223rd Field Co R E.
Vol. 23. (Continued)

Place	Date	Hour	Summary of Events and Information	Remarks and references to Appendices
ECURIE. A27 b. 8. 3.	12.11.17.		The following work carried on (1) New battalion camp at BRAY (2) Improvement to Robert's Camp (3) Model trenches ECOIVRES (4) Divisional canteen ECURIE. RAILHEAD. (Completed 12.11.17). Forward work as follows. Revetting SEVERN in places required. Work on BRITANNIA, Northwards from junction of SEVERN and BRITANNIA. Erecting 4 Elephant shelters for bomb store at BANK STATION. Gumboot store Longwood. Bridge over BRITANNIA (HENIN LIETARD RD) completed 14.11.17.	
			Investigations for ARLEUX - BOIS BERNARD passage still continued. Dug-out at TUNNEL H.Q. continued.	
	14.11.17		Lt BUCHANAN left for four days leave to PARIS. Corps commander inspected men who took part in raid.	
	16-11-17.		Work as above. Major P COCHRAN RE. goes on leave to England handing over the command of the company temporarily to CAPT F W. MOORE RE.	FWM
	18.11.17.		Work as above. Lt R. W. M. BUCHANAN RE rejoins company from PARIS. ROBERTS camp completed.	FWM
	19.11.17 to 22-11-17		Work carried on BATTN camp at BRAY. Model trenches ECOIVRES and on Forward work as above the shelters for BOMB STORE at BANK STATION, NEW GUMBOOT STORE at LONGWOOD were completed 22-11-17. The detachment at BRAY rejoined company on 22-11-17.	FWM
	23-11-17		No work owing to relief of Sections Nos 1+2 relieving 3+4 at RED LINE Dugouts 3+4 return to camp with Hdqrs of company at ECURIE.	FWM
	24-11-17		Forward work as before. Take over completion of CANTEEN at RIDGE ROAD. ROCLINCOURT. and also the GUMBOOT store ROCLINCOURT from 211th Coy RE.	FWM
	25-11-17		Work as above	FWM
	26-11-17		All work as before. Work also commenced by 2/Lt PAGET assisted by 100 men of No 2. Labour Coy. on the COMMANDANTS HOUSE - BAILLEUL ROAD	FWM
	27.11.17 28-11-17		All above work in hand carried on.	FWM
	29-11-17		Lt BARKER leaves coy. on PARIS LEAVE from 30-11-17 to 3-12-17. GUMBOOT STORE + CANTEEN Taken over from 211th Coy completed.	FWM
	30-11-17 to 2-12-17		All work carried on as above. Officers club at ECURIE Mess + kitchen etc taken over from 126th Coy. RE.	FWM
	3-12-17		Major P. Cochran RE returns from leave + takes over command of Coy. from Capt. F.W. Moore RE	FWM

1875 Wt. W593/826 1,000,000 4/15 J.B.C. & A. A.D.S.S./Forms/C. 2118.

Army Form C. 2118.

WAR DIARY
or
INTELLIGENCE SUMMARY.
(*Erase heading not required.*)

Instructions regarding War Diaries and Intelligence Summaries are contained in F. S. Regs., Part II. and the Staff Manual respectively. Title pages will be prepared in manuscript.

223rd Field Co R.E
Vol 23 (Continued).

Place	Date	Hour	Summary of Events and Information	Remarks and references to Appendices
ECURIE A27 b. 8. 3.			The following awards have been gained by the company this month Military Cross Lieut R V M BUCHANAN RE for gallant conduct in connection with a raid. (Routine Orders XIII Corps No 1153 dated 16.11.17) Distinguished Conduct Medal No 98632. 2nd Corpl B. J. JOHNSTON Royal Engineers: for conspicuous gallantry, coolness and initiative during a raid on enemy's trenches. (Routine Orders XIII Corps No 1182 dated 24.11.17.) Military Medals No 98416. Sapper J J GOUGH. R.E for gallant conduct during a daylight raid on the 8th instant (Routine Orders XIII Corps No 1157 dated 17.11.17.) No 98587. 2nd Corpl H. M. STANLEY Royal Engineers: - for conspicuous gallantry and determination during a raid (Routine Orders XIII Corps No 1169 dated 21.11.17) P Cochran Major R.E. O.C. 223rd Field Co R.E	

A7092. Wt. W128.9/M1293. 750,000. 1/17. D. D & L. Ltd. Forms/C2118/14.

ORIGINAL.

Vol 22

CONFIDENTIAL

WAR DIARY

of

223rd Field Company.R.E.

From 1/12/17 to 31/12/17.

VOLUME XXII

==*=*=*

Instructions regarding War Diaries and Intelligence Summaries are contained in F. S. Regs., Part II. and the Staff Manual respectively. Title pages will be prepared in manuscript.

WAR DIARY
or
~~INTELLIGENCE~~ SUMMARY.
(Erase heading not required.)

223rd Field Co. R.E.
Vol 24

Army Form C. 2118.

Place	Date	Hour	Summary of Events and Information	Remarks and references to Appendices
ECURIE. A 27 b. 8.3.	2.12.17.		Major P. Cochran R.E. returned from leave. Weather very cold with frosts. Work continued in trenches by No. 1 & 2 sections. Under orders for move, so no. of men employed in preparing transport. Work on Officers club continued.	
	3.12.17.		Lt. BARKER. R.E. returned from PARIS leave. Cpl J. McFarlane went to Heavy Bridging School AIRE	
	6.12.17.		Handed over forward billets and work to the 416 Field Co. R.E. 56th Division. Company concentrated at ECURIE CAMP.	
ACQ (Billets)	7.12.17.		Marched out of ECURIE CAMP at 9.45 a.m. for ACQ. Reached ACQ at 12.30. Went into billets. So many repairs required. Obtained horse standings but in very poor condition. Had difficulty in finding suitable accomodation.	
	7.12.17.		Captain F. W. MOORE. M.C. R.E. left to attend course for O.C. and 2nd in command of Field Companies at BLENDECQUES.	
	11.12.17.		Lt. W. INGHAM went on leave to ENGLAND. 12th – 26th Lt. R.V.M. BUCHANAN M.C. went to attend camouflage course at WIMEREUX.	
	15.12.17.		Lt. R. V.M. BUCHANAN. M.C. returned from camouflage course.	
	8.12.17. – 17.12.17.		Sections on squad drill & rifle exercises. Lectures. Knotting & lashings. Repairs to horse standings. Putting bunks in large hut 100 completed. Bunking billet 40. Erecting new horse standings ECOIVRE. Improvements to waiting room MONT. ST. ELOI station. Played football in afternoons. Had two company matches. 15 men billetted near at ECURIE and working on Officers Club.	
	20.12.17.		Very hard frost. Prepared transport for the move.	
ECURIE. A 27 b. 8 3	21.12.17.		Moved back to camp at ECURIE. Found camp much as it was left. Roads very slippery but no mishaps with transport. Our forward dug-out handed over as battalion H.Q. We are given Batt H.Q. in ARLEUX – SUGAR FACTORY road. However this cannot be occupied owing to gas. New accomodation being made in VIMY. & VIMY LINE.	
	25.12.17.		Work commenced in line but greatly interfered with by heavy fall of snow. 16 men living in VIMY. LINE.	
	26.12.17		Work on TUNNEL DUGOUT continued, & also passage joining up two entrances at ASHFIELD commenced. Remainder of Section 4 moved up to line. 2nd Lt. PAGET made liason officer with Corps in connection with training scheme.	
	27.12.17.		Frost still continues. Lt. W. INGHAM. R.E. returns from leave	
	28.12.17.		Lt. W. INGHAM. attached C.R.E. as adjutant whilst CAPT. C.K. WALKER away on leave	
	30.12.17.		Lt. BUCHANAN with section 2 moved up to improve accomodation in new forward billets in ARLEUX SUGAR FACTORY RD.	
	30.12.17.		CAPT. F. W. MOORE M.C. R.E. returns from course at BLENDECQUES and takes over command temporarily of 223rd Field Co. R.E.	
	31.12.17.		Frost still continues & work hampered in the line	P. Cochran Major R.E. O.C. 223rd (Field) Coy. R.E.

A7092 Wt. W128 9/M1293 750,000. 1/17. D. D & I. Ltd. Forms/C2118/14.

ORIGINAL.

Vol 23

CONFIDENTIAL.

WAR DIARY

of

223rd Field Company.R.E.

1/1/18 to 31/1/18.

VOLUME XXV.

==*=*=*

Instructions regarding War Diaries and Intelligence Summaries are contained in F. S. Regs., Part II. and the Staff Manual respectively. Title pages will be prepared in manuscript.

WAR DIARY

or

~~INTELLIGENCE SUMMARY.~~

(*Erase heading not required.*)

223rd Field Co R.E.
Vol 25

Army Form C. 2118.

Place	Date	Hour	Summary of Events and Information	Remarks and references to Appendices
ECURIE. A 27 b. 8. 3.	1. 1. 18.		Frosts and cold weather continued. Work continued. No infantry available from Bde	
	3. 1. 18.		Section 4 returned to H. Q. Section I moved up to advanced H. Q under 2nd Lt PAGET. R.E. Work commenced on two strong points W of RED. LINE. 100 infantry of 92nd Bde attached, also two officers. 150 infantry and officers living in VIMY. LIEVIN. LINE. Work on supporting points in ARLEUX continued by Section 2. No infantry available. The following back work carried on by men to ECURIE. W [illegible] two Erection of Soldiers' Kitchen BRUNEHAUT. AREA. Erection of [illegible] hut in camp, also repairs to [illegible] standings.	
			Captain F. W. MOORE. M.C. R.E. returned from 211th Company R.E. MAJOR P. COCHRANE R.E. awarded M.C. in NEW YEAR Honours	
	4. 1. 18.		Lt H. W. COULTAS went on leave to ENGLAND.	
	6. 1. 18.		Thaw set in with heavy rain	
	8. 1. 18.		Froze night of 7. 1. 18	
			Heavy fall of snow. Work impeded.	
	9. 1. 18.		Captain F. W. MOORE. M.C. R.E attached 210th Field Co R.E. for work on CORPS. wiring scheme with 20 sappers Section 3. 1 Section 210th attached for work in back areas. Work continued of on the 3. S. P's behind RED. LINE. also S.P. in ARLEUX. [illegible] TUNNEL and Adv H. Q continued. Rear work continued.	
	14. 1. 18.		LT W. INGHAM returned from C. R. E. on the return of CAPT. G.K. WALKER. from leave.	
			CAPT. F. W. MOORE returned from 210th F. C. R. E.	
	15. 1. 18		Brigade relief no sections relieved & permanent party. Section 2 moved down on night of 14th Section 1 moved down 15th Section 3 from LONGWOOD to ADV. H. Q. Section 4. moved forward. Very heavy rain. Permanent party of 93rd Bde attached 4. Off 100 O. R.	
	16. 1. 18.		Trenches in very bad condition owing to rains. Commenced work on extension of Reading room ECURIE. Remainder of work continued as before. Attached infantry moved from VIMY. LIEVIN. LINE except 1 platoon owing to bad conditions, 1 platoon in front of LONGWOOD. one in ORCHARD. D.O.	
	19. 1. 18.		Lt COULTAS returned from leave.	
	21. 1. 18.		LT. BARKER. proceeded on leave to ENGLAND. Lt BUCHANAN to hospital sick (Scabies). Lt COULTAS and 20 men Section 1 attached 210th F. C. R.E. for work on CORPS wiring scheme. Work commenced on erection of two DETCHET. HUTS. MONT. St ELOY. party billeted there for the purpose. Erection of SODEN KILN. NINE. ELMS. AREA. commenced. Shell slits at D. H. Q. begun.	
	27. 1. 18		Sections relieved. Section 1. from LONGWOOD to adv. H. Q Section 2 to adv. H. Q under 2nd Lt PAGET. Section 3 & 4 moved back to H. Q Brigade relieved.	
	30. 1. 18		Commenced work with 92nd Brigade SAPPING. Co. on new trench from ARLEUX LOOP to BARON	

A7092 Wt. W128 9/M1293 750,000. 1/17. D. D & L Ltd. Forms/C2118/14.

Instructions regarding War Diaries and Intelligence Summaries are contained in F. S. Regs., Part II. and the Staff Manual respectively. Title pages will be prepared in manuscript.

WAR DIARY
or
INTELLIGENCE SUMMARY.
(Erase heading not required.)

223rd Field Co R.E.
Vol 25.

Army Form C. 2118.

Place	Date	Hour	Summary of Events and Information	Remarks and references to Appendices
ECURIE A 27 b.8.3.			Extract from 1st Army Routine Orders 2329. ACT. OF COURAGE. The General Officer Commanding wishes to express his appreciation of the following ACT. OF COURAGE on the part of No 98516, SAPPER. A. J. SYKES ROYAL ENGINEERS:- On 25th December 1917 a pair of horses attached to a G.S. were frightened by shelling and bolted. SAPPER SYKES seeing them approaching, sprang to their heads, and succeeded in bringing them to a standstill thus in all probability preventing a serious accident. A record of the above will be made in the Regimental Conduct Sheet of this man in accordance with para 1919. (XIV) King's Regulations P Cochran Major R.E. O.C. 223rd Field Co RE	

A7092' Wt. W128.9/M1293. 750,000. 1/17. D. D & I. Ltd. Forms/C2118/14.

ORIGINAL.

9/R 24

CONFIDENTIAL.

War Diary

of

223rd Field Company.R.E.

from 1/2/18 to 28/2/18.

VOLUME XXVI.

Instructions regarding War Diaries and Intelligence Summaries are contained in F. S. Regs., Part II. and the Staff Manual respectively. Title pages will be prepared in manuscript.

WAR DIARY
or
INTELLIGENCE SUMMARY.
(*Erase heading not required.*)

323rd Field Co. R.E.
Vol 26

Army Form C. 2118.

Place	Date	Hour	Summary of Events and Information	Remarks and references to Appendices
A27. b. 8. 3.	1.2.18.		The following work in hand, Forward. S.P. ARLEUX. Bunking dug-outs BARON. Improvement of R.A.P. ARLEUX LOOP, U framing and revetting new trench from ARLEUX LOOP to BARON. Revetting S.P's HULL, DURHAM, LEEDS. BACK. New recreation hut MONT ST ELOY. Rifle range BRAY revetting Markers gallery. SOLDER KILN, NINE ELMS area. Making shell slits D.H.Q. The following camps repairs being done. Repairing horse-standings. Building mud walls & digging shell slits. Erecting sheds for cutting up food.	
	3.2.18.		Solder KILN, NINE ELMS area complete.	
	5.2.18.		2nd LT. PAGET. went on leave to ENGLAND 5th–20th. Brigade relief. 93rd came into the line. Sections 1 & 2 moved back and sections 3 & 4 moved up. Only 75 infantry attached instead of 100, owing to one battalion less in Brigade.	
	6.2.18.		LT. H.F. BARKER. returned from leave.	
	9.2.18.		Bunking of dug-outs in BARON completed. A new C.T. commenced from BABY TRENCH to TOMMY TRENCH to avoid low ground. Other work continued.	
	12.2.18.		LT. R.V.M. BUCHANAN. M.C. R.E. returned from C.R.S. Three detachments of 1 officer and 25 O.R. attached for work belonging to COLDSTREAM GUARDS IRISH GUARDS, GRENADIER GUARDS. Detachment of C.G. went up the line for 12 days, also detachment (G.G.) for 6 days. IRISH GUARDS remained in camp. Detachment of 1 officer & 25 O.R. of 13th Y. & L. reported. They remained in camp. Forward [illegible] at SANDBAG, VILLA, ORCHARD [illegible] and TUNNEL.	
	15.2.18.		CAPTAIN F.W. MOORE M.C. RE left for ENGLAND on 30 days leave 16.2.18 – 18.3.18.	
	16.2.18.		LT. R.V.M. BUCHANAN left for hospital (Jaundice). Thus [illegible] taken to 30 C.C.S.	
	17.2.18.		Sub LT. WILLIAMS reported for [illegible] in getting R.E. [illegible]. Sections 1 & 2 relieved sections 3 & 4 in forward work.	
	18.2.18.		LT. H.W. COLETAS left to be attached to the R.F.A. Also two sappers went with him. Detachment (1.G.) relieved G.G. 13th Y.&L. [illegible] 15th W. York	
	19.2.18.		LT. WILLIAMS relieved LT. INGHAM in forward work.	
	21.2.18.		2nd LT. L.F. [illegible] returned from leave & relieved LT. BARKER R.E. in the 24th in forward work. G.G. relieved [illegible] G also the 15th W. Yorks relieved 1 [illegible] D.L.I.	
	25.2.18.		New S.P. ARLEUX at [illegible] commenced. This S.P. was suggested by us before but [illegible] could not agree to it. [illegible]	
	27.2.18.		Infantry detachments ~~reported~~ returned to their units ready for the [illegible]	
	28.2.18.		Wagons cleaned & all preparations made for the [illegible] day. Forward sections returned to camp. Work on S.P's LEEDS, HULL, DURHAM practically complete. [illegible] ARLEUX completed [illegible] with U frames & revetted. New [illegible] TOMMY [illegible]	

P. Cochran
Major RE
O.C. 223rd Field Co RE

A7092 Wt. W128 9/M1293 750,000. 1/17. D. D & L. Ltd. Forms/C2118/14.

31st Divisional Engineers.

WAR
DIARY

223rd FIELD COMPANY R. E.

MARCH 1918

ORIGINAL.

WO 95/25

CONFIDENTIAL.

WAR DIARY

of

223rd Field Company.R.E.

From 1/3/18 to 31/3/18.

VOLUME XXVII

Instructions regarding War Diaries and Intelligence Summaries are contained in F. S. Regs., Part II. and the Staff Manual respectively. Title pages will be prepared in manuscript.

WAR DIARY
or
~~INTELLIGENCE~~ SUMMARY.
(*Erase heading not required.*)

223rd Field Co R.E.

Vol 27

Place	Date	Hour	Summary of Events and Information	Remarks and references to Appendices
AUBREY CAMP A.28.a.2.1.	March 1st		Company moved from old camp ECURIE A.27.a.8.3. to AUBREY CAMP. The new camp was in a very bad state, no [illegible]. Horse lines & Q.M.S. established at ANZIN. Fairly good standings, but not in one place.	
	2nd		Work commenced on CORPS WIRING SCHEME [illegible] work on ST CATHERINE SWITCH and ECURIE defences.	
	3rd		FORT GEORGE & ROCLINCOURT LINE. 2nd Lt. R.V.M. BUCHANAN returned from hospital.	
	4th		Continued [illegible]	
	5th		Commenced work on [illegible] trenches.	
	7th		2nd Lt. R.V.M. BUCHANAN M.C. R.E. [illegible] 8 – 22.3.18.	
	8th		Work continued on CORPS DEFENCE SCHEMES. Work being urgent no rest on Sundays. Large working parties employed.	
	11th		Camp bombarded by 2 13.cm guns, at 11.45 P.M. officers mess & O.C.'s bedroom blown up by a direct hit. No casualties except MAJOR COCHRAN slightly wounded by portion of hut. Remainder of night was passed in the trenches.	
	12th		Camp again shelled but no damage done. Men for the most part sleeping in trenches.	
	14th		LIEUT. W. INGHAM transferred to 210th F.C.R.E. to become second in command of that unit. 2nd LIEUT. EASTON (T.F.) transferred from 210th F.C.R.E. to this unit.	
	16th		2 i/c stores & transport moved from ANZIN to lines and accomodation in 60th Divisional Area. Much better lines and accomodation than at ANZIN. Unfortunately accomodation of lorries [illegible] away from lines.	
	17th + 18th		Company all living at AUBREY CAMP and working on FORT GEORGE – ROCLINCOURT line & ST CATHERINE switch.	[illegible]
	19th 20th + 21st		Do. as above. Capt. F.W. MOORE rejoins Company from leave on 19th.	
BLAIREVILLE		22nd	Received orders at 1 A.M. to embus the dismounted personnel at ECURIE at 6 A.M. & they were carried by bus to BLAIREVILLE where they camped the night. The Transport marched by road to BAILLEUL VAL.	[illegible]
COURCELLET le COMTE		23rd	The Transport rejoined dismounted personnel at BLAIREVILLE at 3 A.M. Major P. COCHRAN M.C. R.E. handed over the command of Coy to CAPT. F.W. MOORE & proceeded on a 30 days special leave to England. The Coy moved to camp between BLAIREVILLE and [illegible] HENDECOURT at 3 P.M. & later having to move again at 9 P.M. to COURCELLES-le-COMTE (in camp).	
		24th	Company digging new Corps line E. side of new main line Railway at COURCELLES, working from 5.45 A.M. to 12 noon. LT. BUCHANAN M.C. R.E. rejoined Coy. from leave.	
DOUCHY Les AYETTE		25th	Received orders at 1 A.M. to pack up & move Transport immediately to DOUCHY LES AYETTE. The dismounted personnel dug on the new line W. of COURCELLE from 1 A.M. to 6 A.M. then marching & rejoining the transport at DOUCHY at 8 A.M. Received orders at 5 P.M. for dismounted personnel to move to line W. of COURCELLE & continue [illegible] S. to ABLAINZEVELLE to be [illegible] of G.O.C. 92nd INF. Bde, until relieved [illegible] to move to MONCHY AU BOIS which they did at 6.20 P.M. arriving at 9 P.M.	[illegible]

A7092 Wt. W125.9/M1293 750,000. 1/17. D. D. & L. Ltd. Forms/C2118/14.

Instructions regarding War Diaries and Intelligence Summaries are contained in F. S. Regs., Part II. and the Staff Manual respectively. Title pages will be prepared in manuscript.

~~WAR DIARY~~ or
~~INTELLIGENCE SUMMARY.~~
(*Erase heading not required.*)

223rd Field Coy. RE.
Vol. 26 (continued)

Place	Date	Hour	Summary of Events and Information	Remarks and references to Appendices
MONCHY au BOIS.	March	26th	Dismounted Personnel ordered to return to the Transport lines by G.O.C. 92nd INF. Bde at 3 A.M. which they did arriving at MONCHY at 6 A.M. Expected further orders all day & stood to [illegible] [illegible], but receiving none, [illegible] [illegible] [illegible] [illegible] a good night.	[initials]
		27th	In morning made reconnaissance of PURPLE line from VALLEY WOOD to 700ˣ S. of QUESNOY Farm with C.R.E. [illegible] [illegible] for [illegible] [illegible]. At 3 P.M. dismounted men paraded for [illegible] marched to PURPLE Line & dug the portion from QUESNOY FARM – BUCQUOY Road to S. Div. Boundary distance 700ˣ. When task was completed about 7 P.M. received orders from the G.O.C. 92nd INF. Bde. to place self & company under orders of MAJOR SPEIGHT R.E. (O.C. 210th Fd. Coy. RE) & report to him at VALLEY WOOD for purpose of supporting Infantry who were hard pressed; reported to Major SPEIGHT [illegible] [illegible] the PURPLE line at VALLEY WOOD all night & day [illegible] in there. The men of coy [illegible] [illegible] [illegible] [illegible] [illegible] [illegible] [illegible] day. The transport moved from MONCHY to BIENVILLERS.	[initials]
BIENVILLERS		28th	At 5.30 A.M. received orders to vacate PURPLE line & move to S.W. corner of ADINFER WOOD arriving at 7.15 A.M. At [illegible] received orders to man the PURPLE line N. of QUESNOY Farm which coy did at 10.30 P.M. [illegible] [illegible] in there during the morning [illegible] [illegible] in the afternoon [illegible] [illegible] 200ˣ [illegible] [illegible] Coy at 5 P.M. At 7 P.M. the coy [illegible] [illegible] [illegible] wet & dark night [illegible] at [illegible] END of the line until midnight.	[initials]
		29th	Rested in early morning & then tried to improve accommodation in PURPLE line till noon [illegible] [illegible] [illegible] for the remainder of day in front of [illegible] end of PURPLE line.	[initials]
		30th	Again commenced [illegible] in front of PURPLE line but had to [illegible] [illegible] [illegible] fire, Sapper [illegible] killed & Sapper BAGNALL being wounded [illegible] [illegible] again in evening & continued [illegible] for about 6 hours.	[initials]
GAUDIEMPRE		31st	Relieved in PURPLE line by the 218th Fd. Coy. RE (32nd Div.) at 3 P.M. & then marched [illegible] to GAUDIEMPRE where the Coy. once more rejoined the Transport which had moved there from BIENVILLERS in the morning.	[initials]

J W Moore Capt. RE
O.C. 223rd Fd. Coy. RE

A7092 Wt. W128 9/M1293 750,000. 1/17. D. D & I. Ltd. Forms/C2118/14.

31st Divisional Engineers

<u>223rd FIELD COMPANY R.E. :;: APRIL 1918.</u>

ORIGINAL.

Vol 26

C O N F I D E N T I A L.

WAR DIARY

of

223rd Field Company.R.E.

From 1/4/18 to 30/4/18.

VOLUME XXVIII

1

Instructions regarding War Diaries and Intelligence Summaries are contained in F. S. Regs., Part II. and the Staff Manual respectively. Title pages will be prepared in manuscript.

WAR DIARY

or

~~INTELLIGENCE SUMMARY.~~

(Erase heading not required.)

223 Field Coy RE

Vol 28

Army Form C. 2118.

Place	Date	Hour	Summary of Events and Information	Remarks and references to Appendices
ORPY	April 1. 1918		Company paraded at 8.30 AM and marched from GOUDIEMPRÉ to ORPY (near IVERGNY) where it went into billets for the night	[initials]
CAUCOURT	" 2. 1918		Company paraded @ 7.45 AM. The transport went independently by road & the dismounted personnel went by busses as far as SAVY & then marched to CAUCOURT where it went into billets	[initials]
	" 3. 1918		Company paraded @ 10 AM for Kit Inspection. Plumbers of No 3 Section repairing baths at CAUCOURT. Tool Carts overhauled & lists of deficiencies made out. Remainder of the day company resting	[initials]
	" 4. 1918		Paraded at 9 AM for Section Drill. Remainder of day spent in cleaning transport vehicles. No 3 Section completed repairs to baths at CAUCOURT & the men were bathed in the afternoon.	[initials]
			CAPT. J.W. MOORE MC RE left the Company to proceed to take over command of the 12th Field Coy RE & handed over the command of the Company to LIEUT H.D. COULTAS RE.	[initials]
	" 5 "		Morning training in Section Drill, Musketry, Gas Drill, Bayonet fighting etc. LIEUTS [illegible] & [illegible] RE visited FREVILLERS MAGNICOURT & HERMIN [illegible] billets	[initials]
	" 6 "		Company training in Section Drill, Musketry, Gas Drill, Bayonet fighting & [illegible] the afternoon recreational training. 6 Carpenters of No 4 Section started erection of Soda Water Factory @ AUBIGNY for XIII CORPS	[initials]
	" 7 "		Morning CHURCH PARADE. Remainder of day Recreational training	[initials]
	" 8 "		Received orders at 11 AM to move to billets at HERMIN. Company paraded @ 2 pm & marched to HERMIN where it went into Billets. 4 Carpenters working at AUBIGNY on SODA WATER FACTORY	[initials]
HERMIN	" 9 "		Company training in Section Drill, Bayonet fighting, Gas Drill. Lectures by Section Officers. 10 Carpenters working at SODA WATER FACTORY. No 2 section making stores for rifle ranges @ CAUCOURT & MAGNICOURT.	[initials]
	" 10 "		SUB-LIEUT WILLIAMS RND left to rejoin the ANSON BATT.	
			Received orders at 1 AM from CRE that Company was to proceed to HAUTEVILLE for work under Engineer-in-Chief 1st ARMY. Also that the OC Company was to meet the CRE @ 8.30 AM to proceed to WAGONLIEU to site trenches & which was done. The Company paraded @ 9 AM & proceeded by road to HAUTEVILLE. — At about 11.30 AM LIEUT BUCHANAN MC RE who was in charge received written orders from a Staff Officer XIII CORPS to halt at AUBIGNY as the Company was going to proceed to the NORTH	[initials]

Instructions regarding War Diaries and Intelligence Summaries are contained in F. S. Regs., Part II. and the Staff Manual respectively. Title pages will be prepared in manuscript.

WAR DIARY
or
~~INTELLIGENCE~~ SUMMARY.
(Erase heading not required.)

223 Field Coy RE
Vol 28.

Army Form C. 2118.

Place	Date	Hour	Summary of Events and Information	Remarks and references to Appendices
	April 10/18.		Orders were first received that the dismounted personnel were to entrain @ VANDELICOURT & proceed to the LILLERS AREA with the 93 Inf. Brigade Group. These orders were cancelled & the dismounted personnel entrained @ VANDELICOURT @ 5 pm & proceeded via LILLERS & ST VENANT & HAZEBROUCK to VIEUX-BERQUIN arriving @ this place @ about 3.30 am where it detrained &	
	" 11/18		came under orders G.O.C. 93 Inf. Brigade. Orders were received from Brigade Major 93 Inf Brigade to march to MERRIS where the Company went into BILLETS @ 6 AM. The transport	MG HAZEBROUCK 5A.
MERRIS	" 11/18		came by road under TRANSPORT OFFICER 93 Inf. Brigade and it arrived @ MERRIS at 6 pm. Orders received from B.M. 93 Inf Brigade to be ready to support the Brigade which was making an attack in the evening of the 11th.	MG
	" 12/18		At 1.30 pm the transport was sent to BORRE. The Company received verbal orders @ about 1.30 pm from B.M. 93 Inf. Brigade to take up a line between MERRIS and OUTTERSTEENE which it did. The G.O.C. 93 Inf Brigade (Brig Genl TAYLOR) then sent Lieut BARKER H.F. RE to reconnoitre OUTTERSTEENE for signs of the enemy. He reported that he had seen 3 (three) whereupon No. 3 Section was sent to try and capture them. It came under heavy M.G. fire & it withdrew to the line in front of the village. The Company also came under M.G. fire from OUTTERSTEENE & @ about 3 pm orders were received from G.O.C. 92nd Brigade (B.Gen WILLIAMS) that the Company had to retire and to take up a position on the high ground to the WEST of MERRIS. This was successfully done and the Company took up a line from F10 central to F6c5.6. and came under the orders of COL. GURNEY who was commanding a composite Battalion of the 92nd BRIGADE. At about 5pm permission was given by COL GURNEY for the Company to withdraw from this line and to come up under the orders of MAJOR MANSELL RE OC 211 Field Coy RE who was responsible for the digging of a new reserve line. The Company withdrew @ 7 pm & dug itself in on a front of 250 x & [illegible] under the 2 in 620 STRAZEELE HAZEBROUCK [5A]	Sheet 36A 1/40000. MG

A7092' Wt. W128 9/M1293. 750,000. 1/17. D. D & L. Ltd. Forms/C2118/14.

3

Instructions regarding War Diaries and Intelligence Summaries are contained in F. S. Regs., Part II. and the Staff Manual respectively. Title pages will be prepared in manuscript.

WAR DIARY
or
~~INTELLIGENCE SUMMARY.~~
(Erase heading not required.)

223 Field Coy R.E.
Vol. 28

Army Form C. 2118.

Place	Date	Hour	Summary of Events and Information	Remarks and references to Appendices
MERRIS	April	12/18.	and was in touch on its right with the 40th Division and on its left with 211 FIELD COY R.E.	
	"	13/18	At about 12.30 A.M. the Company received orders that it was to be relieved. At about 2 A.M. the 93rd L.T.M. Batteries relieved Sections Nos. 1 & 2 who then withdrew to BORRE under command of LIEUT. [illegible] R.E. At about 4.15 A.M. Sections 3 & 4 were relieved by one Platoon of the 6th AUSTRALIAN BATTALION – 2nd AUSTRALIAN DIVISION & these Sections marched to BORRE rejoining Sections 1 & 2. The dismounted personnel then marched to HONDEGHEM to which place the transport had proceeded during night April 12/13. Company went into billets at HONDEGHEM & reported its arrival to C.R.E. 31 DIVISION under whose orders it came again	
HONDEGHEM.	"	14/18.	Company refitting awaiting orders. 2nd LIEUTS J. R. GRANT R.E. & A.P. [illegible] R.E. reported for duty with the Company. 5 O.R. as reinforcements	
	"	15/18	Company paraded @ 9 A.M. for Kit Inspection. Officers lectured their sections on 'Demolitions'. Order received that the unit was under one hours notice to move.	
	"	16/18.	O.C. Company reconnoitred the HAZEBROUCK defences with CRE 31 Division. The Company lectured by Section Officers on various subjects. Remainder of day Company resting.	
	"	17/18.	Company paraded @ 8.30 A.M. for work. They marched to BORRE where they worked on the [illegible] TRENCH of the HAZEBROUCK DEFENCES (W.12.d.1.2 to V.30.d.5.5). TRENCH traced out. 2 Strong points started [illegible] on 40 [illegible].	27 Sheet 1/40000
	"	18/18.	Officers reconnoitring trenches of HAZEBROUCK DEFENCES for bridging purposes. In afternoon sections 1.3 & 4 put up 22 foot bridges over 10 gaps for communications in HAZEBROUCK DEFENCE SYSTEM.	
AU SOUVERAIN	"	19/18	Received orders @ 4 A.M. that Company was to move into billets @ AU SOUVERAIN. Company paraded @ 9.15 A.M. & arrived @ AU SOUVERAIN where it went into billets. In afternoon No 2 Section erected a trestle bridge over the CANAL (HAZEBROUCK – LA MOTTE) @ D.18.c.6.8. Length of bridge 45'0". No 1 Section unloading Bridging lorries arriving from No 8 PONTOON PARK. Officers reconnoitring the 31st DIVISIONAL AREA for BRIDGING Purposes.	
	"	20/18	Company paraded @ 8 o'clock A.M. No 1 Section making good roadway between D.30.a.14 & D.16.b.6.0. "2 " cutting gaps for wheeled traffic to make through passage from E.14.b.2.8 – E.13.c.2.8 – D.23.b.6.7 – D.24 [illegible]	

A7092 Wt. W128 9/M1293 750,000. 1/17. D. D & I. Ltd. Forms/C2118/14.

Instructions regarding War Diaries and Intelligence Summaries are contained in F. S. Regs., Part II. and the Staff Manual respectively. Title pages will be prepared in manuscript.

WAR DIARY
or
~~INTELLIGENCE SUMMARY.~~
(Erase heading not required.)

223 Field Coy R.E.
Vol. 28.

Army Form C. 2118.

Place	Date	Hour	Summary of Events and Information	Remarks and references to Appendices
AU SOUVERAIN	April 20/18.		No 3 Section making 2 footbridges over stream between E26 Central & K2a3.3. No 4 Section working on trestle bridge @ D17b4.8. No 2 Section prepared trestle bridge @ D18c6.3 for demolition.	
	" 21/18.		No 1 Section working with party of 13th Y&L Battn on trenches from Pte SEC BOIS to Pte MARQUETTE & from GRANDE MARQUETTE FARM to D18b9.3 with 15th W. YORKS BATT. Lts [illegible] & GRANT reconnoitred the Reserve LINE from Pte SEC BOIS to Pte MARQUETTE. No 2 Section erected foot bridge @ D18a15.25 across canal of 45'0". No 3 Section finished foot bridge @ E25d8.5. No [illegible] Sapper SYKES wounded by shell fire. No 4 Section erecting Trestle Bridge & making Plank Track @ D17b4.8. Foot bridges also erected at E9b1.3 — E1b3.4 — E1a6.2.	Ref. Reference Sheet 36A N.E. 1/20000.
	" 22/18		No 3 Section working on TRESTLE BRIDGE @ D17b4.8. 4th trestle launched. 12 G.S. Wagon loads of material from BOIS de NIEPPE. FOOTBRIDGE @ D18a15.25 prepared for demolition. No 1 Section supervising wiring trench (RESERVE SUPPORT) from Pte SEC BOIS to Pte MARQUETTE. Party of 200 13 Y&L Battn digging. 350x trench dug 300x wire. No 2 Section wiring SUPPORT LINE from E15b1.9 to E4c4.3 (RAILWAY) 350x Double Apron wire put out & 1550 Yds of wire pickets. No: Sapper RIPER wounded. Party of 80 of 18 D.L.I carrying. No 4 Section supervising & digging trench in Pte SEC BOIS 400x dug. Party of 100 18th D.L.I. No. SAPPER BROOK wounded	
	" 23/18.		No 3 Section working on HEAVY TRESTLE BRIDGE @ D17b4.8. Completed to 3 Bays decking. Another 60x Plank track made up to it. 20 Inf of 13 Y&L assisting. 12 G.S. wagon loads of planking brought from BOIS NIEPPE. Afternoon horse lines shelled by Shrapnel. No: Sapper NEWTON killed. No. Sapper QUAYLE wounded & No. Driver [illegible] wounded. Nine horses also wounded. Horse lines moved to D7a5.8. No 1 Section @ night with 403 of 13 Y&L digging trench between E3d & E4a. 1078 Yds trench dug to 1st trace — R.E. put up 300x wire. No 2 Section with 80 Carrying party of 10th E. YORKS wiring support line from E9d0.1 to E4c4.3. 480x double apron wire erected. Also pickets out for another 600x. No 4 Section supervising digging of Pte SEC BOIS strong point. Parties digging 'C' Coy of S.G Battn Tanks and 1 Coy 18th D.L.I. 540x of 36" Breastwork half completed.	

A7092 Wt. W128 9/M1293 750,000. 1/17. D. D & L. Ltd. Forms/C2118/14.

5

Army Form C. 2118.

Instructions regarding War Diaries and Intelligence Summaries are contained in F. S. Regs., Part II. and the Staff Manual respectively. Title pages will be prepared in manuscript.

WAR DIARY

or

~~INTELLIGENCE SUMMARY.~~

(Erase heading not required.)

223 Field Coy RE

Vol 28

Place	Date	Hour	Summary of Events and Information	Remarks and references to Appendices
N. SOUVERAIN	April	24/18	No 3 Section paraded @ 8am. Parties of 20 OR from 13th Y.L. Also 6 G.S. wagons for carrying material from BOIS de NIEPPE. All labour on HEAVY TRAFFIC @ D17 b 4.8. Cleaning of bridge completed. Standards for handrails also erected & 60x of Roadway completed – 60x of side bearers laid.	[initials]
	—	25.	Major P. COCHRAN. R.E. returned from leave and took over command of Company. Work continued Sections 1,2,3,4 on night work. Section 2 on SUPPORT LINE. Section 1 on Reserve line. Section 3 on Bridge D17 b 4.8 Section 4 on 1st SEC. BOIS defences. Sappers engaged on wiring & supervising construction of breastworks	
	—	26	Work continued. Notice boards made & erected.	
HUTMENTS V8 D 3.4. 1 mile S of HONDEGHEM	—	27	Bridge at D17 b 4.8 completed. Company moved at 1 pm to hutments at V 8 d 3.4. Very comfortable camp. Mounted Section only in canvas.	
	—	28	Company had holiday. All kit inspected & gas respirator drill. Company under 1 hours notice to move.	
	—	29.	Work commenced on 1st line B. ZONE. HAZEBROUCK defences. 4 Sections less 8 men on work, tool carts cleaned & repaired, also bicycles. 200 men of the [illegible] B.de as working party. Work consists principally of improving & making good the existing lines. In many places a new line has to be cut owing to the trench being taken too deep. Work carried on in four portions of the line. Each section having its allotted portion, 2nd Lt [illegible] working with Section 1, 2nd Lt [illegible] with Section 4. Lt [illegible] BARKER supervising camp work and the cleaning of waggons.	

P. Cochran
Major RE
O.C. 223rd Field Co RE

A7092 Wt. W128.9/M1293 750,000. 1/17. D. D & L. Ltd. Forms/C2118/14.

ORIGINAL.

WO 95/27 [handwritten]

C O N F I D E N T I A L.

WAR DIARY

of

223rd Field Company.R.E.

from 1/5/18 to 31/5/18.

VOLUME ~~XXVIII~~ XX/X.

Instructions regarding War Diaries and Intelligence Summaries are contained in F. S. Regs., Part II. and the Staff Manual respectively. Title pages will be prepared in manuscript.

WAR DIARY
or
~~INTELLIGENCE SUMMARY.~~
(Erase heading not required.)

223rd Field Company R.E.
Vol 28.

Army Form C. 2118.

Place	Date	Hour	Summary of Events and Information	Remarks and references to Appendices
HUTMENTS. V8d 3.4 ½ mile S of HONDEGHEM.	1st MAY.		Work continued on B. LINE. HAZEBROUCK defences. Breastwork being constructed in four different portions of line. Working party of 200 men GUARDS. B^de daily. Company stores being cleaned and sorted. Limber wagons being painted.	
			2nd Lt EASTON with 4 sappers went to 5th Army Musketry Course.	
	2nd		Works continued on B. LINE and fair progress made. Commenced placing E. Shelters in barns.	
	1			
	7th		2nd Lt EASTON and 4 sappers ~~[illegible]~~ returned from 5th Army Musketry Course.	
	8th		Received orders to prepare to take over line opposite METEREN from 1st AUSTRALIAN. DIV. Lt BUCHANAN and 2nd Lt EASTON sent to look over line and take over work of 1st AUSTRALIAN. F.C.O.	
	9th		Company less ½ Section 3 and TRANSPORT. move up to ROUKLOSHILLE. N.E. of FLETRE. Accommodation in small bivouacs along hedge side close to cottage. Cellar in cottage suitable for occupation. Had 4 G.S. waggons up that night with stores. Enemy sent over three shells, ~~the~~ one of which burst close to gate and 2Lt H.F. BARKER. R.E. was wounded. A fleshwound just above the wrist. No definite work taken over, as there seemed to be no system. Only 1 B^de 93rd B^de in the line. Section 3 joined remainder of company on 10th.	
	10th		Company divided up as follows. Section I. FONTAINE HOUCK. S.P. Section 2. Strengthening houses and guarding mines. Section 3. BELSACE. F^me ½ Section 4. PHINCBOOM. S.P.	
			Had the following transport up each night to supply dump at BELSACE. F^me 4 G.S. waggons and 3 limber wagons.	
	11th		Sapper work consisted of wiring and thinning hedges	
	14/15th		Commenced work on two S.P.'s one situated at HAUTE. PORTE. F^me which Section 3 carried on with, the other at FONTAINE. HOUCK. SOUTH. a post in conjunction with the FRENCH on our left.	
	15/16th		92nd B^de relieved 93rd B^de but Field Company remained the same. Work continued the same, but certain infantry companies of the D.L.I. were made responsible for the digging of the S.P.'s This allowed all the Sappers to be employed on their own work. All parties worked well.	
	16th		Dr KIRBY killed by A.A. shell over HONDEGHEM.	
	17		C.S.M. DRAKE went on 3 days leave to ENGLAND.	
	18		Commenced new R^t BATT. H.Q. in FLETRE. METEREN. ROAD. An A.E. shelter let into the bank. All material obtained from a derelict mobile workshop opposite.	
	18th		Sap WILLOUGHBY wounded shell.	
	20th		Work completed on HAUTE. PORTE. F^me S.P	

Instructions regarding War Diaries and Intelligence Summaries are contained in F. S. Regs., Part II. and the Staff Manual respectively. Title pages will be prepared in manuscript.

WAR DIARY
or
INTELLIGENCE SUMMARY.
(Erase heading not required.)

Army Form C. 2118.

223rd Field Company R.E.

Vol 28.

Place	Date	Hour	Summary of Events and Information	Remarks and references to Appendices
ROUKLOSHILLE R31d 4.1. Transport lines. V8d 3.4.	21st May 1918		Forward billets heavily shelled & shells dropping close no doubt intended for a battery. Shelling on road intermittent throughout the day. The following casualties all slightly wounded. Sap BARKER. A. Sap KIRSOP A.E. Sap. LOWTHER J.H. Sap SKAIFE J who was guarding one of the mules, wounded (gas.) 93rd Bde relieved 92nd Bde. Owing to the wishes of G.O.C. working parties not night of relief. Work joining different portions of SUPPORT LINE making continuous trench around S.P.s PHINEROOM & BELSACE Fm. Parties of 600 asked for which would have completed this work. However parties only consisted of 350.	
	22nd		A continuous trench completed along SUPPORT LINE, also around BELSACE FARM & PHINEROOM. Wiring completed around BELSACE one belt, & also all round FONTAINE HOUCK SOUTH S.P. Forward billets shelled but no casualties. Advance party of relieving company 64th arrived to take over. After work on night 22/23 Company less 2Lt BUCHANAN and 9 O.R. left to hand over, marched down to R.E. DUMP LA BREARDE where buses had been erected. Company embussed at LA BREARDE + at 2.30 a.m. and debussed at RACQUINGHEM	
RACQUINGHEM	23rd		Transport moved off at 9 a.m. independently. Marched into ORCHARD CAMP. All men under canvas. Well arranged camp with plenty of room for games.	
	24th		Kit inspection. 2Lt BUCHANAN and party rejoined company night of 24/25.	
	25th		Men had holiday. 2nd Lt. PAGET went to gas course at WISQUES.	
	26th		Church parade service.	
	27th		Training Physical Drill, Musketry.	
	28th		120 of the company inoculated.	
	29th		Off duty through inoculation. 19 reinforcements arrived.	
	30th			
	31st		Training Physical Drill, ~~Musketry~~, ceremonial practice parade with 93rd Bde. Parade quite good except ground too small. Company drawn up in column of sections. March past in file repeated by the band	

P. Cochran
Major R.E.
O.C. 223rd Field Coy R.E.

A7092 Wt. W128 9/M1293 750,000. 1/17. D. D & L. Ltd. Forms/C2118/14.

ORIGINAL.
==*=*=*

Vol 28

CONFIDENTIAL.
==*=*=*=*=*

WAR DIARY

of

223rd Field Company.R.E.

From 1st June to 30th June,1918.

VOLUME ~~XXIX~~ XXX

Army Form C. 2118.

WAR DIARY

~~or~~

~~INTELLIGENCE SUMMARY.~~

(Erase heading not required.)

Instructions regarding War Diaries and Intelligence Summaries are contained in F. S. Regs., Part II. and the Staff Manual respectively. Title pages will be prepared in manuscript.

223rd Field Company R.E.
Vol 30.

Place	Date	Hour	Summary of Events and Information	Remarks and references to Appendices
RACQUINGHEM	1. 6. 18.		Training continued. Practised at ceremonial. Musketry. 2nd Lt L. F. PAGET. returned from Gas school NISQUES.	
	2. 6. 18		Church parade	
	3. 6. 18		Transport inspected in the morning, along with Bde transport by G.O.C. 31st Division.	
	3. 6. 18		Company dismounted took part in ceremonial parade with 93rd Bde. Inspected by G.O.C. 2nd Army. Marched past along road sport by the massed bands who played too fast	
	4. 6. 18		Training resumed. Musketry on range at A. 24. in afternoon. Company inspected by C.R.E.	
	5. 6. 18		Musketry on range No 1 & 2 sections. Sec 3 & 4. Squad & rifle drill. Knotting & lashing & map reading arrived.	
	6. 6. 18		Coy sports. Much enjoyed by all concerned. Very keen competition.	
			Sections 1 & 2 bridging. Sections 3 & 4 Musketry on range.	
	7. 6. 18.		Section 3 & 4 bridging. Section 1 & 2 + best shots from 3 & 4 on range.	
	8. 6. 18.		Training continued in morning. Had inter-company rifle meeting in afternoon. 211th, 1st, 210th, 2nd 223rd 3rd Company led on grouping & deliberate but came down in Rapid. Knock out competition won by us. Spr FENWICK 3rd best shot. Shooting very good.	
	9. 6. 18		Had church parade with battalion EAST. LANCS. Lt BUCHANAN went to MUSKETRY COURSE LUMBRES.	
	10. 6. 18.		Divisional R.E. sports. Company did very well in running events. Won inter-company relay race. Spr BUSHEL No 4. Section won individual prize for winning most events. No success in the mounted events. Had heavy rain for ¾ hr during luncheon interval.	
	11. 6. 18		Route march. Did inter-section scheme, defence of the villages of COUBRONNE, LE RONS and QUIESTÈDE. Sappers took great interest in scheme and the majority of reports were very good.	
	12. 6. 18		Training continued. Pontooning & musketry. Influenza broke out in the company, commencing amongst the drivers.	
	13. 6. 18		Sappers assisting in horse lines.	
	14. 6. 18		Received warning order to be ready to move up to line. Capt COULTAS. went on reconnaissance with Brigade MAJOR	
	15. 6. 18		Under orders to move. Packed up & marched off at 4.30 P.M. Men wearing full marching order. Marched with 93rd Bde 2/Bde through CAMPAGNE, RENESCURE, STAPLE, to our destination situated 700 yds S of HONDEGHEM V9 a 1.7. arrived in camp at 10.15 P.M. Men billeted in barns. Officers in tents. Roads very dusty and march slow. 23 men sent to hospital suffering from influenza. Most of these drivers	
HONDEGHEM.	16. 6. 18.		In camp, standing by. Several more drivers down with influenza. 4 Sappers per section detailed for horse-line duties. These sappers took charge of their own section animals. In morning these sappers were all mounted for practice.	

A7092 Wt. W128.9/M1293. 750,000. 1/17. D. D & L. Ltd. Forms/C2118/14.

Army Form C. 2118.

Instructions regarding War Diaries and Intelligence Summaries are contained in F. S. Regs., Part II. and the Staff Manual respectively. Title pages will be prepared in manuscript.

WAR DIARY
or
~~INTELLIGENCE SUMMARY.~~
(Erase heading not required.)

223rd Field Company R.E.
Vol 30 (Continued)

Place	Date	Hour	Summary of Events and Information	Remarks and references to Appendices
HONDEGHEM	17.6.18.		Under orders to move back to RACQUINGHEM. Orders changed at 4 P.M. to accompany 93rd Bde group to the vicinity of SERCUS for work under XV th Corps. Moved off at 8. P.M. at 10.15 P.M. halted on roadside outside SERCUS, awaiting orders as to location of camp. Received word at 10.45. and moved into large farm to spend the night as no camp was prepared. Men billeted in barns and very comfortable. Officers in farm house. Horse lines in fields at the back. Sappers drove tool-carts & between the trestle waggon. 20 evacuated to hospital.	
EEK HOUT. CASSEL.	18.6.18.		Drew tents and erected them in field at the back. Only 16 tents available. Went round EAST. HAZEBROUCK line and took over portion from 145. A. T. Co. R.E. Line taken over ran just EAST of HAZEBROUCK station to LA KREULE. Work very interesting as it was in the neighbourhood of houses. This line reconnoitred by officers in the afternoon.	
	19.6.18.		Work commenced on EAST. HAZEBROUCK line. No infantry parties available. Section 3 made foot bridge across canal.	
		1.30 P.M.	Warning order received from BRIGADE that Division were taking over line from 29th Division on 20/21st	
	20.6.18	2. a.m.	Received orders from C.R.E. to take over work from 455th F. Co R.E and billets from 497th F. C. R.E. CAPT. H.W. COULTAS with	
		9. a.m.	Took over work from 455 F. C. R.E. in LEFT. Bde area. 2nd Lt BADDELEY and GRANT went round work. Took over demolitions at PETIT. SEC. BOIS and three mines at SPEARMINT. CORNER. Advance party took over billets of 497 at AU. SOUVERAIN. and round HAZEBROUCK GARAGE and transport lines at LA CUNEWELE.	
HAZEBROUCK. GARAGE.		2.15 a.m.	Marched up to AU. SOUVERAIN. with sappers available. Sick remained at Transport lines. Only 60 men available for work. Each section had its own billets. Sections 1 & 3 in shelters behind railway embankment. Section 2 in cellars at HAZEBROUCK GARAGE station. Section 4 in a trench situated just South of road. Men very comfortable.	
	21.6.18		Commenced work in line. Section 3 on concrete shelter at Bde H.Qrs and a new battn H.Q in PETIT. SEC. BOIS. Section 4 on PETIT SEC. BOIS. Section 2 on RESERVE. LINE. Section 1 in SWARTENBROUCK. No men available from Bde.	
	22.6.18		Visit from C. R. E. Orders for the company to move back and commence work on new D. H. Q. Our work in line to be taken over by 210th F. Co R. E. Lt. BUCHANAN returned from Musketry Course LUMBRES.	
	23.6.18.		Company less 10 men moved back by trestle waggons to ~~[illegible]~~ commence work on new D. H. Q. 2nd Lt BUCHANAN in charge of this work. 26 infantry attached for this purpose & brought their tents. 6 tents drawn for the accomodation of the company in transport lines. 10 men and H. Q. established at B. 9 b. 5. 4. At H. Q. there is an engine and band-saw. Men living in small shelters along hedge side. Took over from 210th F. Co RE work on roads leading to LA. MOTTE.	
D 9 b. 5. 4.	24.6.18.		Work continued on D. H. Q.	

A7092 Wt. W128.9/M1293. 750,000. 1/17. D. D & L. Ltd. Forms/C2118/14.

Instructions regarding War Diaries and Intelligence Summaries are contained in F. S. Regs., Part II. and the Staff Manual respectively. Title pages will be prepared in manuscript.

WAR DIARY
or
~~INTELLIGENCE SUMMARY.~~
(Erase heading not required.)

Army Form C. 2118.

223rd Field Company R.E
Vol 30 (Continued) 3

Place	Date	Hour	Summary of Events and Information	Remarks and references to Appendices
	25.6.18		Work continued on D.H.Q.	
D9b.5.4. S of HAZEBROUCK.	26.6.18		Section 4. (12 men) made new entrance to shelter at EAST end of NIEPPE FOREST. Shelter made suitable for R.A.P. Work completed in day took 13 hours. Model trenches constructed for operations. Notice boards for same.	
	27.6.18		Work continued on D.H.Q. roads repaired where necessary. Bridge repaired at PAPOTE +	
	28.6.18 29.6.18 30.6.18		Work on D.H.Q. delayed through lack of material.	
			The following awards have been gained by the Company this month:–	
			Birthday Honours	
			Distinguished Conduct Medal No 98405. Sapper (A/Lce Cpl) DRAKE T.	
			Mentioned in Despatches for distinguished and gallant service and devotion to duty during the period 25.9.17. to 24.2.18 (London Gazette 21st May 1918.) 98625 2nd Corpl (A/Corpl) J. McFARLANE.	
			Immediate Award	
			Military Medal No 46287 L/Cpl. W. EPTON.	

P Cochran
Major RE
O.C. 223rd Field Co RE

A7092 Wt. W128.9/M1293. 750,000. 1/17. D. D & L. Ltd. Forms/C2118/14.

ORIGINAL.

CONFIDENTIAL

WAR DIARY

of

223rd Field Company.R.E.

From 1/7/18 to 31/7/18.

VOLUME XXXI

Instructions regarding War Diaries and Intelligence Summaries are contained in F. S. Regs., Part II. and the Staff Manual respectively. Title pages will be prepared in manuscript.

WAR DIARY
or
~~INTELLIGENCE~~ SUMMARY.

(Erase heading not required.)

Army Form C. 2118.

223rd Field Company R. E.

Vol 31.

Place	Date	Hour	Summary of Events and Information	Remarks and references to Appendices
S of HAZEBROUCK d 9 b. 5. 4.	1. 7. 18.		2nd Lt EASTON. A. and 4 O. R. went to 2nd Army Rest Camp. AUDRESSELLES.	
	2.		Work continued on D. H. Q. All outside work finished by 3rd and the division moved in.	
	3		Making stretcher racks for light railway trucks.	
	4.		Commenced work on M. G. E. for M. G. C. at SANITAS CORNER in a house	
	5.		new A. D. S. erecting two elephant shelters 26 ft long. Excavation done by R. A. M. C.	
	6th		2nd Lt. GRANT and Corp APPLEYARD. went to R. E. Training school ROUEN. Three weeks course.	
			Work continued	
	9th		Commenced construction of two DE. MOIR. pillboxes. in AVAL. WOOD.	
	10th		Received orders to take over work in R I B 2nd area from 211th F. C. R. E	
	11th		Took over demolitions Section 4. proceeding to live in LA MOTTE for this purpose, also work at Bn H Qrs on five elephant shelters at FETTLE FARM. Continued work on Pill boxes and A. D. S. Work on D. H. Q. handed over to 211th F. C. R. E. CAPT. H. W. COULTAS went to rest-hostel HARDELOT. Lt BUCHANAN left to join 211th F. C. R. E. as second in command	
	12th 13th		Work continued Commenced work on new Batt. H. Q's	
	14th		2nd LIEUT. A. W. ROGERS reported for duty.	
	16th		2nd LIEUT. EASTON returned from 2nd Army Rest Camp. AUDRESSELLES.	
	17th		Two pill-boxes completed. Work commenced on Main Line of Resistance. Sappers employed on A frames & laying trench boards. Other work continued.	
	18th 19th		Work continued commenced erection of 3rd pill-box.	
	20th			
	21st		CAPT H. W. COULTAS returned from rest-hostel. HARDELOT.	
	22nd		Took over work from 210th F. C. R. E on VOLLEY FARM. CORLEY COTTAGE Switch. 350 infantry employed building up breastwork	
			Work continued on Main Line of Resistance now called 2 line. 3rd erection of 3rd Pill box completed.	
	26th		Work on A. D. S. & Brigade H. Q.	
	27th		2nd Lt. PAGET to hospital sick (Influenza)	
			Corpl RODGERS (No3 Section) won 1st prize for best shot at LEWIS GUN. Course 2nd Army S of M.	
	30th		2nd Lt BADDELEY to hospital sick (Scalded hand)	

J. Cochrane Major RE
O. C 223rd Field Co RE

A7092 Wt. W128 9/M1293 750,000 1/17. D. D & L. Ltd. Forms/C2118/14.

ORIGINAL.

9R30

CONFIDENTIAL.

WAR DIARY

of

223rd Field Company. R.E.

From 1/8/18 to 31/8/18.

VOLUME XXXII.

==*=*

Instructions regarding War Diaries and Intelligence Summaries are contained in F. S. Regs., Part II. and the Staff Manual respectively. Title pages will be prepared in manuscript.

WAR DIARY
or
~~INTELLIGENCE SUMMARY.~~
(*Erase heading not required.*)

Army Form C. 2118.

223rd Field Co. R. E.

Vol 32.

Place	Date	Hour	Summary of Events and Information	Remarks and references to Appendices
S of HAZEBROUCK D9b.5.4	1.8.18.		Work continued on COBLEY COTTAGE VOLLEY FARM switch and 2 line. Work consisted in building up parapets, [illegible], clearing brushwood, fixing A frames, trench boarding, and erecting B.E. shelters. Section 4 [illegible] demolitions at LA MOTTE. Section [illegible] still in A.D.S. By means of close liaison good work has been done by the garrison working in their own time.	
	2.8.18		Sap UPCHURCH wounded whilst coming through LA MOTTE	
	4.8.18		2Lt GRANT returned from R.E. training school ROUEN.	
	7.8.18		2nd Lt PAGET returned from hospital.	
	9.8.18		2Lt W. B. MITCHELL joined company from R.E. base depot. Leave allotment of 5 men every three days. Strength of company much reduced [illegible] away at 2nd army rest camps	
	10.8.18 13.8.18 14.8.18		Work continued. Section 3 relieved Section 4 in demolitions. 2nd Lt ROGERS took over work on 2 line. 2nd Lt PAGET [illegible] at LA MOTTE 2 men went on leave to PARIS.	
	14.8.18		120th Bde (40th Division) took over right sector. This Bde attached for instruction.	
	15.8.18.		Work continued the same, only no working parties available from 93rd Bde owing to operations. VIEUX BERQUIN occupied.	
	18.8.18.		OUTTERSTEENE ridge captured & operations continued by us in the shape of fighting patrols.	
	20.8.18.		No working parties at all, so work held up.	
	22.8.18		Handed over work to 229th Field Co R.E. 40th Division, & took officers round.	
W. of FLETRE W4d 4.4.	23.8.18		Left S of HAZEBROUCK & moved to MELLINS FARM just W of FLETRE. Took over work from 95th Field Co R.E. Officers in cottage and men in shelters in B. line. Sections 1 & 2 moved forward to shelters at LES ORMES	
	24.8.18.		Work commenced on Batt H.Q.s but what was handed over. Improving forward & back billets. Shelters being put in for officers.	
	25.8.18		Ditto.	
	26.8.18.		Divisional Horse Show. Came out third.	
	27.8.18		Improved accomodation forward & back billets.	
	28.8.18.		Commenced work on 2 line with 2 companies of 93rd Bde. Commenced clearing berm [illegible] through METEREN. Handed over mines & work on Batt H.Q to 497 F.C. R.E. 29th Division (alteration of Divisional Boundary)	

A7092 Wt. W128 9/M1293 750,000. 1/17. D. D & L. Ltd. Forms/C2118/14.

Instructions regarding War Diaries and Intelligence Summaries are contained in F. S. Regs., Part II. and the Staff Manual respectively. Title pages will be prepared in manuscript.

WAR DIARY
or
INTELLIGENCE SUMMARY.
(Erase heading not required.)

223rd Field Co RE
Vol 32.

Army Form C. 2118.

Place	Date	Hour	Summary of Events and Information	Remarks and references to Appendices
W of FLETRE	29.8.18		Work continued on 2 line wiring at night & clearing berm. 1 Section on notice boards & track billets.	
N4 d 4.4.	30.8.18		Work continued by 2 sections in the morning on 2 line. Enemy retired and BAILLEUL. 3 Section of Company made bridge across BECQUE just W of BAILLEUL. 2 craters also revetted & filled. Work done in 4 hours & transport crossed that night. Work commenced at 6 PM & was completed at 10.	
LES. ORMES. W of METEREN	31.8.18.		Company moved forward to forward billets LES. ORMES. Reconnoitred roads & tracks around BAILLEUL. Division squeezed out & 29th Division took over front. Advance continued.	

P. Cochran
Major R.E.
O.C. 223rd Field Co RE

A7092 Wt. W128:9/M1293 750,000. 1/17. D. D & I. Ltd. Forms/C2118/14.

ORIGINAL.

9182 31

CONFIDENTIAL.

WAR DIARY

of

223rd Field Company.R.E.

From 1st Sept. to 30th Sept.1918.

VOLUME XXXII

==*

Instructions regarding War Diaries and Intelligence Summaries are contained in F. S. Regs., Part II. and the Staff Manual respectively. Title pages will be prepared in manuscript.

WAR DIARY
or
INTELLIGENCE SUMMARY.
(*Erase heading not required.*)

223rd Field Co R.E.
Vol 32.

Army Form C. 2118.

Place	Date	Hour	Summary of Events and Information	Remarks and references to Appendices
LES. ORMES. W. of METEREN.	1. 9. 18.		Company employed on making limber track and improving road around S of BAILLEUL by BAILLEUL station.	
	2. 9. 18.		Work on road continued, also commenced erection of water point at BAILLEUL station.	
	3. 9. 18.		Making Corduroy track around crater on STEINWERCK Rd. Completed. Drew bridging material. 2nd Lt A. F. BADDELEY returned from hospital.	
S.E. BAILLEUL. S.27.C.7.5.	4. 9. 18.		4 Sections moved forward into camp just S.E of BAILLEUL. Mounted section & heavy waggons left W of BAILLEUL. Work on plank road round crater E of on main BAILLEUL. ARMENTIERES road. Improved bridges & widened them. 2nd Lt A. F. BADDELEY went back to hospital.	
	5. 9. 18 –		Work continued on tracks & began to work on new Adv D. H. Q at S. 30 a. 0. 3 Put up NISSEN HUT 94 Armstrong, also repaired two huts. Erecting Office at BAILLEUL STATION. R.E. Dumps. Heavy waggons moved forward.	
	9. 9. 18.		Working in conjunction with 9 2nd Bde in line, who required very little assistance.	
	10. 9. 18		Work continued the same.	
	12. 9. 18		SAPPER. [illegible] wounded in assisting R.F.A. whose billet had been struck. CAPT. H. W. [illegible] went on leave to ENGLAND: 13-27th	
	13. 9. 18.		Commenced work on constructing camp. Took over work on water supply from 210th F. C. RE and 455 FIELD. CO. RE. for winter. Completing sleeper dumps on PLOEGSTEERT. Rd. Commenced horse standings.	
	16. 9. 18 –		Commenced new Bde H. Q. at LAMPERNISSE Fm. and support Bde H. Q in BAILLEUL.	Camp [illegible] shelled by night, but no damage [illegible]
	20. 9. 18		Work continued the same	
	21. 9. 18.		[illegible]	
	22. 9. 18.			
	23. 9. 18.		In preparation for an advance Section 1 & 2 employed on night work constructing two sleeper tracks round craters on LE ROMARIN. PLOEGSTEERT. Rd. 2 platoons of D. Coy 12 ROYAL [illegible] assisted. Work completed in 4 hours.	
	24. 9. 18 –		Work continued by 3 & 4 on LAMPERNISSE FARM. Had working party of 150 in two shifts of 50. 8 shelters erected with gas frames, 2 actually covered complete. Bde moved in on the 27th.	
	27. 9. 18		Section 1 continued work on support Bde. Section 2 employed on camp work & [illegible] for the formation of forward dumps at LE. DON.	
	27. 9. 18.		Commenced erection of baby elephants for forward camp in S. 30. b.	

A7092 Wt. W12S9/M1293 750,000. 1/17. D. D & L. Ltd. Forms/C2118/14.

Instructions regarding War Diaries and Intelligence Summaries are contained in F. S. Regs., Part II. and the Staff Manual respectively. Title pages will be prepared in manuscript.

WAR DIARY
or
~~INTELLIGENCE SUMMARY.~~

(Erase heading not required.)

Army Form C. 2118.

223rd Field Co R.E.
Vol 32

Place	Date	Hour	Summary of Events and Information	Remarks and references to Appendices
T.30 b.4.2 EAST of BAILLEUL.	28.9.18.		Parade of No 1 & 2 sections at 6.30 a.m. to move forward to camp at T.30 b.4.2. Very wet morning. Spent day in completing & improving accommodation. CAPT. H.W. COULTAS returned from leave. Section 3 moved forward at [illegible] 5.45 P.M. Received orders by telephone from C.R.E. that two sections had to pack up and move off complete with a mobile column formed of the 93rd Inf Bde. Sections 1 & 2 detailed. 6 P.M. C.R.E. arrived and gave orders that O.C. was to go too & act as S.O. to Brigadier. Section 4 & all mounted personnel & H.Q. moved forward. 8.30 P.M. the following moved off to join mobile column O.C. Sections 1 & 2 complete with transport, 1 trestle waggon containing 6 infantry bridges I.S. 2 trestle waggons each containing one trestle & 2 bays [illegible] (1 trestle waggon borrowed from 210th Field Co R.E.). Column was stopped by 1 trestle waggon being ditched. However [illegible] cleared off [illegible] column	
	29.9.18		In NEUVE EGLISE – DRANOUTRE road [illegible] road was blocked with troops & transport. Transport was [illegible] through to join the ADVANCE GUARD. Section limbers & 2 trestle waggons remained with Main guard with the Bde Transport. Column advanced without a halt until arriving just [illegible] side of [illegible] when it came under shell-fire and gas. Brigadier ordered all transport back, but Sappers proceeded. Column proceeded on until ROSSIGNOL was reached when there was a halt after [illegible] in the [illegible] just after leaving ROSSIGNOL column came under M.G. fire from MESSINES and shell fire from the direction of ARMENTIERES. SAPPERS and PIONEERS fell out of column 300 yds past ROSSIGNOL with orders to clear roads & fill up the shell holes over the ground that we had passed, also to make the detour round the crater at BAKERY Crossroads. Several shell holes filled but work seriously impeded by shell fire. At 4.45 a.m. commenced clearing a track around southern edge of crater at BAKERY + Sappers took on the [illegible] as only 20 shovels were available. At 5.15 a.m. the enemy put a barrage down on BAKERY crossroads. Several Sappers took refuge in the crater. Unfortunately a shell dropped in the crater. Total casualties 2 killed 1 died of wounds and 11 wounded (2 remained at duty). No stretcher bearers available so men had to be helped back. Pioneers then resumed the work as soon as situation permitted. Track suitable for limbers & guns completed by 7.30 a.m. Reports transmitted to C.R.E. at 8.30 a.m. [illegible]	½ coy of D.C.L.I. [illegible] attached

A7092 Wt. W128 9/M1293 750,000. 1/17. D. D & L. Ltd. Forms/C2118/14.

Instructions regarding War Diaries and Intelligence Summaries are contained in F. S. Regs., Part II. and the Staff Manual respectively. Title pages will be prepared in manuscript.

WAR DIARY
or
INTELLIGENCE SUMMARY.
(Erase heading not required.)

Army Form C. 2118.

223rd Field Co. R.E.

Vol 32. (3)

Place	Date	Hour	Summary of Events and Information	Remarks and references to Appendices
U 14. a. & b. S of MESSINES.	29.9.18.		Remained in close proximity to road [illegible]. Unable to approach [illegible] enemy [illegible] fire. Also transport not available. Found a little accommodation in shelters in an old trench. Rain came on. [illegible] up so were able to have tea, but no hot food for men. Three Officers slept the night in a small shelter [illegible] high but [illegible]. Very dark night so did not commence work on the road [illegible].	
	30.9.18.		Up at 5.15 a.m. Commenced work around tank traps at U 14 b. [illegible] road from old track. Work completed by 9 a.m. Returned to the place where we had spent the night & the cooks had a very good breakfast ready for us. Very wet morning & everybody soaked. However things were better after the [illegible]. In afternoon moved into trenches at UNUSUAL POST much better accommodation. [illegible] the afternoon & we got the road through [illegible] front line [illegible]. 1 N.C.O. of GERMAN found in new campaign 1 anti-tank rifle.	
	29/30		No 4 Section & 1 platoon K.O.Y.L.I. put timber track round crater @ T 27 c 3.2. Work completed.	
	30		No 3 Section & 1 platoon K.O.Y.L.I. repaired road between T 29. c 3.2. & [illegible]. Road made good for limbers.	
			Nos 3 & 4 sections & transport moved forward to T.16 [illegible] and [illegible] mobile column had stopped [illegible] of the L.Y.S.	

[illegible]
Major R.E.
O.C. 223rd Field Co. R.E.

A7092 Wt. W128_9/M1293. 750,000. 1/17. D. D & L. Ltd. Forms/C2118/14.

ORIGINAL.

Vol 32

CONFIDENTIAL.

WAR DIARY

of

223rd Field Company.R.E.

From 1/10/18 to 31/10/18.

VOLUME ~~XXXIII~~ XXXIV

==*

Army Form C. 2118.

WAR DIARY
or
INTELLIGENCE SUMMARY.
(Erase heading not required.)

223rd Field Co R.E.
Vol 33

Instructions regarding War Diaries and Intelligence Summaries are contained in F. S. Regs., Part II. and the Staff Manual respectively. Title pages will be prepared in manuscript.

Place	Date	Hour	Summary of Events and Information	Remarks and references to Appendices
ADV. CAMP at U 14. b. 5. 8. Transport lines at T16 b. 2. 8.	1st. 10. 18.		Sects. working material for improvement of track round back [illegible] U 14 b. No. 4 preparing material for [illegible] Ark crater. Sections 1 & 2 moved back to transport lines and 3 & 4 came forward. 2nd Lt. EASTON proceeded on leave to England. 3rd – 17th	D. Coy. 13 K.R.? still working [illegible]
	2. 10. 18.		Improvement to approaches to timber track. Section 3 & 4 on timber track around ASH CRATER & [illegible] completed. Work continually interrupted by shell fire & finally stopped owing to him setting fire to a dump. Sign of [illegible] in there had been disclosed by the 211th working there in broad daylight. 2nd Lt. L. F. PAGET went on leave to ENGLAND 4th–18th	
	3. 10. 18.		Improvement to approaches to timber track. Sappers standing by ready to bridge the LYS. Sections at transport lines employed in getting up material to transport lines. 6 C.S.M. MITCHELL & 2 sappers went out [illegible] to reconnoitre river & follow patrol over the river. However patrol never [illegible] back owing to the [illegible] of the enemy. Got back to camp at 6.30 a.m.	
HILL 63.	4. 10. 18		Moved into the huts recently built by the enemy on HILL 63 these huts to be repaired for [illegible] Very good accommodation.	
U15 a 5. 9	5. 10. 18		Commenced repair of these huts. Section 1 moved up from transport lines. [illegible] very comfortable & work [illegible] most interesting	
	6. 10. 18		Work continued on Hill 63. Section 1 remained at horse-lines. Horse lines shelled, [illegible] wounded	
	11. 10. 18		2nd Lt. ROGERS returned from PARIS leave.	
	13. 10. 18		2nd Lt. GRANT went on leave to ENGLAND. 14th–28th	
	14. 10. 18		Work continued on D.H.Q. All sappers concentrated on H.F.A. hut. [illegible] completed	
	15. 10. 18.		Work continued on D.H.Q. Personnel of G. branch moved in. Capt. COULTAS returned to horse lines. 6 C.S.M. MITCHELL [illegible] with 210th. All moved into adjacent shelters and tents & left huts for D.H.Q.	
HILL 63 Nr PLOEGSTEERT.	16. 10. 18.		Division moved up. Completed G & Q offices. Section 3 worked from 6 a.m. to 5.30 P.M. Section 4 was in reserve and at 12.5 a.m. was sent to assist 210th F.C. on construction of bridge over LYS at WARNETON. All bridging gear sent up & the [illegible] bridge which [illegible] at 12 noon 3 hours before that of the other companies. Bridge completed at 4 P.M. Section 4 [illegible] in their good work by 6 C. 210th F. C. C.S.M. at 12 noon went off to ERQUINGHEM [illegible] pontoon waggon to bridge [illegible] at PONT ROUGE. He got back at 4 a.m. after getting the material to its destination.	

A7092 Wt. W128:9/M1293 750,000. 1/17. D. D & L. Ltd. Forms/C2118/14.

Instructions regarding War Diaries and Intelligence Summaries are contained in F. S. Regs., Part II. and the Staff Manual respectively. Title pages will be prepared in manuscript.

WAR DIARY
or
~~INTELLIGENCE SUMMARY.~~
(~~Erase heading not required.~~)

Army Form C. 2118.

223rd Field Co R.E.
Vol 33.

Place	Date	Hour	Summary of Events and Information	Remarks and references to Appendices
HILL 63.	17.10.18.		Section 2 conferring 1 battalion of infantry on PLOEGSTEERT. WARNETON RD. Section 1. Loading party for road material. Sections 3 & 4 in D. H. Q & resting. Horse lines moved up to HILL 63. and company altogether.	
WARNETON	18.10.18.		Company moved to WARNETON and went into huts & shelters near old GERMAN ammunition dump. Men very comfortable and horses on metalled road. Section 2 on road again with 1 battalion infantry. Sec 1 camp. Sec 4 took over charge of WARNETON. B23 Sec 3 under C.S.M. DRAKE moved to PONT ROUGE and took over bridge there.	
RUBAIX. FILATURE DU NORD.	19.10.18.		Marched from WARNETON to RUBAIX via QUESNOY. CRE altered destination on the route. Company marched well and was complimented by Divisional Commander. Flags flying along the route and given a hearty welcome by the civilians. Billeted in the factory. Men very comfortable and horses had good hard standing. Inhabitants most obliging and gave me every attention.	
RUBAIX on banks of the canal de RUBAIX.	20.10.18.		Constructed a bridge to take 17 tons over canal between TURCOING and RUBAIX. Improved existing bridge and made it capable of taking 6 tons. Work completed that evening. Corpl RAY (No 1 section) Sapper BALL (No 2 Section) missing, there being no trace of them. 2nd Lt EASTON and PAGET rejoined company from leave. Men in comfortable warehouse for the night. Section 4, moved to LANNOY to be attached to 93rd Bde and found them at NECHIN. Company moved from factory to the bank of the canal to be near site of work.	
LANNOY. RUE DU BOIS.	21.10.18.		Constructed bridge to take 6 tons over canal at A26. a 5. 1 (Sheet 37) between RUBAIX and WATTRELOS. Company moved to LANNOY. C.S.M. and 4 sappers sent on motor lorry back to HILL 63 to fetch material for light bridges. Material taken right up to the bank of the L'ESCAUT at PECQ. Corporal A.S.C killed and driver wounded however lorry was driven back to Bde H.Q. material undamaged. 2nd Lt ROGERS & section 4 amidst heavy shell fire constructed a footbridge across L'ESCAUT at PECQ. Bridge consisted of barrels and ladders lashed together.	
NECHIN.	22.10.18.		Company moved to NECHIN. Further reconnaissance made for constructing traffic bridge over L'ESCAUT. Transport lines remained at LANNOY.	
PECQ.	23.10.18.		Company in afternoon moved to PECQ. Transport lines to GIBRALTAR. Section was left at NECHIN. All preparations made to build a trestle bridge over L'ESCAUT. Work stopped owing to enemy's activity. Enemy attempted a raid at bridge head and put down a very heavy barrage. 2 Coys. ROYS 1. attached for this work. Company in cellars of a factory. Men quite comfortable.	
NECHIN.	24.10.18.		2 Sections moved back to NECHIN. 2 remained at PECQ. No work possible again as the infantry could not establish an outpost line owing to the presence of the enemy. Received warning order re the move up NORTH.	

A7092 Wt. W128_9/M1293. 750,000. 1/17. D. D & L. Ltd. Forms/C2118/14.

Army Form C. 2118.

WAR DIARY
or
INTELLIGENCE SUMMARY.
(Erase heading not required.)

Instructions regarding War Diaries and Intelligence Summaries are contained in F. S. Regs., Part II. and the Staff Manual respectively. Title pages will be prepared in manuscript.

223rd Field Co R.E.
Vol 33

Place	Date	Hour	Summary of Events and Information	Remarks and references to Appendices
NECHIN	25.10.18		Sections 2 + 3 brought down from RECQ to NECHIN. All preparations made to move. 1 Section 229th Field Company arrived to take over.	
MOUSCRON	26.10.18		Moved off at 1.15 from NECHIN. Marched via LEERS, WATTRELOS. Roads all setts the whole way. Arrived at MOUSCRON at 5.15 and went into billets near the station. No 78296 SAPPER W. CHESWIN awarded the MILITARY MEDAL 3.11.18	
do.	27.10.18		Company remained at MOUSCRON. Day spent resting.	
STACEGHEM	28.10.18		Company paraded at 8.30 Am & marched to STACEGHEM where it went into Billets. [initials] Major P. COCHRAN M.C. RE proceeded on leave to England & handed over acting command of company to Capt [illegible] RE	
do	29.10.18		Sections 1.2 & 3 forming 31st Div RE dump at I 20 d 4.2: material for corduroy road found & chiefly also making accommodation for Dump Staff. [initials] Secn 4 drawing in Weldon Trestle Bridging Equipment from bridge at H 21 b 8.0. [initials]	Sheet 29 Belgium & France
do	30.10.18		Secns 1.2 at working at 31 Div RE Dump @ I 20 d 4.2 Putting in more corduroy. Secn 3 doing trestle drill [initials] 2nd Lt J.K. RE returned from leave to England.	
do	31.10.18		Standing by for orders. Bridging equipment & wagons attached to 210 FIELD COY RE. [initials] Secn 4 working at 31 Div RE dump [initials]	

[signature] Capt RE
O/C 223 Field Coy R.E.

A7092 Wt. W128 9/M1293 750,000. 1/17. D. D & L. Ltd. Forms/C2118/14.

ORIGINAL.

NWC 33

CONFIDENTIAL.

WAR DIARY

of

223rd Field Company.R.E.

From 1/11/18 to 30/11/18.

Volume XXXV

Instructions regarding War Diaries and Intelligence Summaries are contained in F. S. Regs., Part II. and the Staff Manual respectively. Title pages will be prepared in manuscript.

WAR DIARY
or
~~INTELLIGENCE SUMMARY.~~
(Erase heading not required.)

Army Form C. 2118.

223 FIELD COY RE
VOL 36

Place	Date	Hour	Summary of Events and Information	Remarks and references to Appendices
STACEGHEM.	Nov 1/18		Company standing by for orders. Bridging equipment returned from 210 Field Coy RE.	
"	2/18		Cleaning wagons etc. recreation in afternoon.	
HALLUIN	" 3/18		Company paraded 21.07.10 and marched with 93 Inf Bgde Group to HALLUIN where unit went into billets	
"	" 4/18		All sections on pontoon drill in the morning. Recreational training in the afternoon.	
"	5/18		Sections 1, 2 & 3 pontoon drill during the morning & recreation in the afternoon. No 4 section proceeded to RONCQS for the day & completed seating in cinema for the 93rd Inf Bgde. 183 No 6 CSM Drake left to join the 162nd Division as RSM.	
"	6/18		LIEUT. W.B. MITCHELL R.E. proceeded on leave to PARIS. Notified by APM ROUBAIX that the bodies of CPL RAY & Sapper BALL had been found in the canal at ROUBAIX. The Company paraded at 11.30 AM in wet weather & marched to STACEGHEM where we went into billets.	
STACEGHEM	" 7/18		The 4 sections making light footbridges of collapsible boats at the XIX CORPS RE Dump. L/CPL BRADLEY & SAPPER ELDERMAN received the Military Medal. 22 Petrol Tin piers & 12 Boats made.	
"	8/18		No 3 Section paraded @ 8 AM & went to billets @ OOTEGHEM. No 3 Section working in the line with 92nd Inf Brigade. In the evening 2/LT L. PAGET RE went out with a patrol of the 11th E. Lancs Regt to reconnoitre the R. SCHELDT at RUGGE.	
			Sections 1, 2 & 4 making light bridges at XIX CORPS RE Dump. 2 Petrol Tin Bridges 120' long completed & 32 collapsible boats	
OOTEGHEM & RUGGE.	" 9/18.		Received orders at 0800 to move to OOTEGHEM at once. Company marched at 0430 after the men had had breakfast marched to OOTEGHEM. At 0700 word received that the enemy was clearing from positions on the R. SCHELDT. No 3 Section collected a light bridge from 92 Bgde HQ & the Company's transport ... R. SCHELDT. No 3 Section collected a light bridge from 92 Bgde H.Q. ... at RUGGE at 1400 ... down to RUGGE. Here it was put across the river. Sections 2 & 4 ... They put a pontoon bridge 105'0" long over the River, bridging equipment of the 210, 211 & 223 Field Coys R.E. They put a corduroy track 60'0 long at the EAST SCHELDT at RUGGE. After this sections 2, 3 & 4 ... The Company went into ... billets @ RUGGE. SIDE of the bridge. All men worked splendidly. CSM BARNEY RE Section 1 brought light bridges to RUGGE from STACEGHEM by motor lorry. C.S.M. ... from 411 Field Coy RE joined the unit as C.S.M.	
RUGGE.	" 10/18		2/LT ROGERS proceeded on leave to ENGLAND. Trestle wagons carrying corduroy material from ... & site of pontoon bridge & sections completed a corduroy track 115' long at the East side of bridge. ... conveyed the thanks of the GOC 31 Div to the company for the previous day's work.	
RUYEN.	" 11/18		Company by reliefs guarding the pontoon bridge. The company moved across the river to billets in RUYEN. 7 Footbridges across the river SCHELDT @ RUGGE dismantled and material stacked on E. Bank ... RE	
"	~~/18~~			

A7092 Wt. W128.9/M1293 750,000. 1/17. D. D & L. Ltd. Forms/C2118/14.

Instructions regarding War Diaries and Intelligence Summaries are contained in F. S. Regs., Part II. and the Staff Manual respectively. Title pages will be prepared in manuscript.

WAR DIARY
or
~~INTELLIGENCE SUMMARY.~~
(Erase heading not required.)

Army Form C. 2118.

223 Field Coy RE
Vol 35

Place	Date	Hour	Summary of Events and Information	Remarks and references to Appendices
RUYEN.	Nov 12/18		Company guarding pontoon bridge by reliefs. Remainder of time spent resting.	
"	" 13/18		do.	
AVELGHEM	" 14/18		Company paraded @ 08.00 and dismantled the pontoon bridge [illegible]. Paraded again @ 13.00 marched with 93 Inf Brigade group to billets in AVELGHEM.	
LAUWE	" 15/18		Company paraded @ 09.00 [illegible] with 93 Inf Brigade Group to LAUWE where [illegible] went into billets. Major P. COCHRAN R.E. [illegible] from [illegible] Company [illegible] over command of the Company.	
LAUWE.	" 15/18		Billets not very good and sappers sleeping on stone floors. Cleaning wagons and checking bridging gear. In afternoon men played football.	
	16/18		Rifle drill, improvement to billets and cleaning gear & checking stores. Played football match against the R.S.F's and got beaten by 4 goals to nil. Team not in good condition and did not play well together.	
	17/18		Commenced ceremonial drill for G.O.C's inspection. Drivers also on parade.	
	18/18		Practice drill continued. Bunking billets. Reconnaissance done on billets of 93rd Bde & 92nd Bde	
	19/18		Drill continued. Played football against 210th F. C R.E. Won 2 goals to 1.	
	20/18		2 Platoons of KOYLI. employed on getting timber from bank of canal up to dump at WEVELGHEM. Section 1 preparing billets for themselves at R.E. DUMP, WEVELGHEM.	
	21/18		Section 1. moved over to dump at WEVELGHEM & commenced work on making furniture. Practice of ceremonial drill continued. Lt MITCHELL returned from PARIS leave.	
	22/18		Capt H. W. COULTAS and four sappers went on leave to PARIS. All N.C.O. in company received lecture on Demobilisation from Capt FERENS 10 EAST YORKS. Received orders to move on the following day to the St OMER area. All wagons packed in afternoon.	
MENIN	23/18		Left LAUWE at 10.30 a.m. & had slow march as unable to enter MENIN until 12 noon. Went to billets. Sappers in school & officers in empty house. Horses in very good GERMAN stable.	

A7092 Wt. W128:9/M1293 750,000. 1/17. D.D & L. Ltd. Forms/C2118/14.

Instructions regarding War Diaries and Intelligence Summaries are contained in F. S. Regs., Part II. and the Staff Manual respectively. Title pages will be prepared in manuscript.

WAR DIARY
or
~~INTELLIGENCE SUMMARY.~~
(Erase heading not required.)

Army Form C. 2118.

223rd Field Co R.E.
Vol 34

Place	Date	Hour	Summary of Events and Information	Remarks and references to Appendices
YPRES.	24.11.18		Left MENIN at 09.50 and marched over ridges passed GHELVELT and HOOGE Road very loose in parts. Had no difficulties with waggons. The attached motor lorry took cookers on so as to have meals ready on arrival. Accomodation very poor as all houses destroyed. Everyone slept in dug-outs and cellars. Horses had lines amongst the ruins of the old houses.	
STEENVORDE.	25.11.18		Left YPRES at 08.45 and marched via POPERINGHE. Roads fairly good. Had one hour halt on the way. Arrived in billets at 3 P.M. Men very comfortable. Animals had lines in an open field. Fortunately weather was fine. March a very good one and a good pace kept throughout. Units well spaced along the road.	
ARQUES.	26.11.18		Left STEENVORDE at 8.15 a.m. and marched right through. Had no halt for lunch. Roads very good and men marched well. Very heavy [illegible] round CASSEL. Arrived in billets at 2 P.M. Billets very good for the Sappers. Officers very comfortable. Horses in open field.	
"	27.11.18.		Moved horse lines into Supply depot sheds, also drivers into the huts opposite. Made beds for the officers of 18 D.L.I. Repaired baths at ARQUES. Motor lorry still used for getting material from dump. FORT ROUGE	
"	28.11.18		Making furniture for 18th D.L.I. improvements to Sappers billets. 2nd Lt A.W. ROGERS M.C. R.E. returned from ENGLISH LEAVE.	
"	29.11.18. 30.11.18		} Improvement to billets continued. The following Honours gained this month. 2nd Lt A.W. ROGERS. MILITARY CROSS. No 140159. SAPPER F. ALDERMAN. MILITARY MEDAL No 98629. L/cpl G.N. BRADLEY. " "	

P. Cochran
Major R.E.
O.C. 223rd Field Co R.E.

A7092 Wt. W12839/M1293 750,000. 1/17. D. D & L. Ltd. Forms/C2118/14.

ORIGINAL.

WO 34

CONFIDENTIAL.

WAR DIARY

of

223rd Field Company. R.E.

From 1/12/18 to 31/12/18.

VOLUME XXXVI

Instructions regarding War Diaries and Intelligence Summaries are contained in F. S. Regs., Part II. and the Staff Manual respectively. Title pages will be prepared in manuscript.

WAR DIARY
or
~~INTELLIGENCE SUMMARY.~~
(Erase heading not required.)

Army Form C. 2118.

223rd Field Co R.E.
Vol 35.

Place	Date	Hour	Summary of Events and Information	Remarks and references to Appendices
ARQUES.	1.12.18.		Construction & improvement of billets. Work being carried on for 15th W. YORKS 18. D.L. 1. & No 3 Coy train.	
			Work continued. Assistance also given 13th YSL. Commenced construction of tables for education	
	7.12.18.		Rehearsal for G.O.C's parade on Longuesse Aerodrome.	
	9.12.18.		Divisional R.E. association trial at MALHOVE.	
	10.12.18.		Last rehearsal for G.O.C's parade.	
	11.12.18.		Divisional R.E. Rugby trial the company played a team picked from 210th & 211th Coys. Result we won by 3 points.	
	14.12.18.		Divisional R.E. inspected by G.O.C and medal ribbons presented. The following from this company received ribbons. MAJOR. P. COCHRAN. M.C. 2nd Lt A.W. ROGERS. M.C. Sergt A. CHAPMAN. M.M. Cpl EPTON. M.M. Cpl FLETCHER. M.S.M. Cpl BRADLEY. M.M. Sap. ALDERMAN. M.M.	
	15.12.18.		Company played R.O.D MALHOVE at association football. We won 3 goals to 1. Lt MITCHELL went on leave to ENGLAND 15.12.18 – 31.12.18	
	16.12.18		Construction of tables continued. Repairs to billets of 15th West Yorks. Improvement to horse-standings.	
	21.12.18		Played Rugby football against 15th West Yorks lost by 2 points.	
	24.12.18		Company concert.	
	28.12.18		Corp. STANLEY. Corp. RAMSDEN. Pion MARSHALL. A. D. LEWIS left unit for demobilisation. Section under 2nd Lt EATON moved to THEROUANNE to divide the huts. Had working party of 150 WEST YORKS.	
	31.12.18.		Lt MITCHELL returned from leave. Lance corporal J.T. FLETCHER awarded CROIX DE GUERRE (French)	

P Cochran
Major R.E.
O.C. 223rd Field Co RE

A7092. Wt. W128.9/M1293. 750,000. 1/17. D. D & L. Ltd. Forms/C2118/14.

31

Vol 35

W A R   D I A R Y .

of the

2 2 3 rd. F I E L D   C O M P A N Y   R. E.

for the month of J A N U A R Y. 1 9 1 9 .

V O L U M E 37.

Army Form C. 2118.

Instructions regarding War Diaries and Intelligence Summaries are contained in F. S. Regs., Part II. and the Staff Manual respectively. Title pages will be prepared in manuscript.

WAR DIARY
or
~~INTELLIGENCE SUMMARY.~~
(Erase heading not required.)

223rd Field Co R.E.
Vol 37.

Place	Date	Hour	Summary of Events and Information	Remarks and references to Appendices
ARQUES.	1/1/19.		Section I still at THEROUANNE. Making forms & tables & preparing for move.	
St OMER.	3/1/19		Lt PAGET. left Company to report WAR OFFICE for duty in N. RUSSIA. Section 3 & H.Q. moved to St OMER and took over camp of 942 Artizan Co. Very comfortable camp with every convenience.	
"	4/1/19		Sections 2 & 4 leaving a guard over billets came to new camp. Lt MITCHELL [illegible] 2nd Lt STEWART Stores Officer at C.R.E.'s office.	
"			Section 3 working on the shops. 2 & 4 employed around camp & making alterations to officers mess.	
	9/1/19		MAJOR R. COCHRAN M.C. R.E. awarded BELGIAN CROIX DE GUERRE.	
	10/1/19.		One section went per motor lorry to BOULOGNE for the day.	
	14/1/19.		Commenced work on Horse staging camp. ARQUES. 1½ sections R.E. and 300 inf party. Building billets for D.L.I. Erection of hospital NISSEN HUT for ~~[illegible]~~ 1/5th WEST YORKS.	
	17/1/19.		Received assistance from 245 Army troops at Horse Staging Camp. 20 men. This party on erection of the necessary NISSEN HUTS. Also 15 sappers from 210th F.C.R.E.	
	20/1/19		Infantry working party increased to 800 & the work continued.	
	22/1/19		Lt EASTON. [illegible] for VRON D'AVAL party of 8 left to complete work.	
	27/1/19		Capt A.W. COULTAS left Company for Demobilisation. The following officers and men awarded Divisional Commanders Badge for good work. Capt A.W. COULTAS. LIEUT. L.F. PAGET. No 98361. Sergt. L. LONSDALE. No 86[illegible]. Sergt. A. WELBOURN. No 98510. Sergt. H. BUCKLE. No 98528 2nd Cpl. J.S. MELLOR. No. 98384. Sapper. [illegible]INSON. No 98513 Sapper. S. MARSHALL. No 98516. Sapper A.J. SYKES. No 98635 Sapper M. BRAYSHAW. No 92454. [illegible] C.R. YARLETT. No 98571. Corpl. J. APPLEYARD.	
			11. Light draught horses marked Y left for CALAIS.	
	28.1.19.		Orders received at 2.15 a.m. to send one section complete to CALAIS along with the remainder of DIVISION. Men paraded at 6 a.m. & marched to station. Lt MITCHELL and Lt EASTON went in charge. Section transport went by road with the transport of 92nd Bde. This party went to [illegible] but were not called upon for duty.	
	31.1.19		Section from CALAIS returned at 9.45 P.M. 1 Light Draught Horse marked Y left for CALAIS.	
	28/1/19		Work at ARQUES carried on by a party from 210th & 150 German prisoners.	
	31/1/19.		45 men demobolised in month of JANUARY.	Cochran Major R.E. O.C. 223rd Field Co R.E.

A7092). Wt. W12839/M1293. 750,000. 1/17. D. D & L., Ltd. Forms/C2118/14.

Vol 36

WAR DIARY.

223rd FIELD COMPANY, ROYAL ENGINEERS.

FEBRUARY, 1919.

Instructions regarding War Diaries and Intelligence Summaries are contained in F. S. Regs., Part II. and the Staff Manual respectively. Title pages will be prepared in manuscript.

WAR DIARY
or
~~INTELLIGENCE SUMMARY.~~
(Erase heading not required.)

Army Form C. 2118.

223rd Field. Co. R.E.
Vol 38.

Place	Date	Hour	Summary of Events and Information	Remarks and references to Appendices
St OMER.	1.2.19		Work continued at V Army Horse staging camp Arques. Working party of 150 P.O.W. obtained.	
	2.2.19.		2nd Lt J.K. GRANT. left company for demobilization.	
			Owing to demobilization of so many drivers, Sappers sent to assist in horse lines.	
	6.2.19.		Lt EASTON left company for demobilization. 9 men left for demobilization.	
	7.2.19.		7 men demobilized.	
	8.2.19		9 " " " Severe frost commenced. Party of 200 Chinamen working at ARQUES instead of P.O.W.	
	9.2.19		9 men demobilized. Work continued at ARQUES and also men working in workshops.	
	10.2.19		30 men demobilized. Company down to a strength of 78 ration strength 68. Cadre formed of retainable personnel.	
	11.2.19 – 17.2.19		Work continued. Numerous demands for repairs of water pipes owing to thaw. Increased labour of 80 P.O.W. & 100 infantry at ARQUES.	
	19.2.19		20 Z horses sent to ARQUES V Horse STAGING CAMP. Accomodation at V Army H.S.C. completed for 600 animals. Trouble with the water supply.	
	20.2.19 – 28.2.19		Work continued on V Army H.S.C. P.O.W. labour reduced to 30. Accomodation completed for 1000 horses. All roads laid with concrete blocks. Commenced on table standing in 10th	Ration strength on 28.2.19. 4.35 [illegible] 65 2 [illegible] 8 riders 18 draught [illegible]

P. Cochran
Major R.E.
O.C. 223rd Field Co R.E.

A7092). Wt. W12839/M1293 750,000. 1/17. D. D & L., Ltd. Forms/C2118/14.

Instructions regarding War Diaries and Intelligence Summaries are contained in F. S. Regs., Part II. and the Staff Manual respectively. Title pages will be prepared in manuscript.

WAR DIARY
or
~~INTELLIGENCE SUMMARY.~~
(Erase heading not required.)

Army Form C. 2118.

223rd Field Co R.E.
Vol 38

V/8 37

Place	Date	Hour	Summary of Events and Information	Remarks and references to Appendices
St OMER.	1/3/19		Work continued at 5th Army Staging camp & work completed on 19/3/19. All outstanding & finished & concrete water troughs.	
	19/3/19		Completed valuation of huts of the following areas Lambres, Isquerdes & Arques.	
	20/3/19		Major P. Cochran R.E. left company & handed over command 475th Field Co. to Lt Mitchell R.E.	
			2nd Lt A.W. Rogers R.E. left company to join 11th Field Co.	P.C. [initials]
	25.3.19.		Five men left for demobilization.	
	26.3.19		"Extract from 31st Divisional Routine orders. 25.3.19. 4386. Decoration Militaire (2nd Class) and Croix de Guerre 98621 Pte. A/L.-Cpl. J.T. Fletcher 223rd FIELD Coy. R.E	
	26.2.19		31st D.A.C. Commenced moving out Transport to WIZERNES. 1 N.C.O. & 6 O.R. went as guard.	
	27.2.19.		D.A.C. completed moving of Transport.	Ration Strength. 31.3.19. 1 officer & 60 O.R. 2 riders 2 L.D. mules.

[signature]
Lieut R.E.(T.)
O.C. 223rd Field Coy. R.E

Army Form C. 2118.

223rd FIELD Coy. R.E.

Vol. 39

Instructions regarding War Diaries and Intelligence Summaries are contained in F. S. Regs., Part II. and the Staff Manual respectively. Title pages will be prepared in manuscript.

WAR DIARY

or

~~INTELLIGENCE SUMMARY.~~

(Erase heading not required.)

Place	Date	Hour	Summary of Events and Information	Remarks and references to Appendices
St. Omer.	1.4.19.		16 O.R. NON-RELEASABLES left for 62nd (HIGHLAND) Division.	
	14.4.19.		1 (X) Horse Rider sent to 5th Army A.C.C. ARQUES.	
				Ration Strength 30.4.19. 1 officer 44 O.R. 1 Rider 2 L.D. mules

[signature]
Lieut. R.E.
O.C. 223rd
FIELD Coy. R.E.

A7092). Wt. W12839/M1293. 750,000. 1/17. D. D & L., Ltd. Forms/C2118/14.

www.ingramcontent.com/pod-product-compliance
Lightning Source LLC
Chambersburg PA
CBHW081436160426
43193CB00013B/2294